WHAT NOW??!!

Moving Past the Election of 2016!

The Jeremiah Letters - Volume 1

By Christopher Gore

Contact the Author

Light Bearer Publishing Company
Attn: Christopher A. Gore
579 Groundhog Lane; Smyrna, DE 19977
lightbearer@gmx.com

ISBN #: 978-0-9861572-8-8

For Worldwide Distribution, Printed in the U.S.A.

Edited by:

Kathryn R. Gore

&

Priscilla A. Gore

Acknowledgments:

Unto my Lord and Savior Jesus Christ; who has endued the knowledge and strength to finish this project for His glory. Unto my lovely wife; Kathryn, your love, your backing, and your support has made the difference in my life. Unto my Dad for giving me your love for politics... unto my Mom for giving me your love for the Bible... unto Rev. Barbara Lynch, my pastor, mentor and friend for encouraging me to serve our Heavenly Father with all my heart... unto my friends, Brett & Nancy Connell for sharing your knowledge of this craft with me... unto the Remnant who is standing strong in the midst of tough times... and unto everyone else who stood with me through the years of my growth and development in Christ.

Thank you!

Dedicated with love unto…

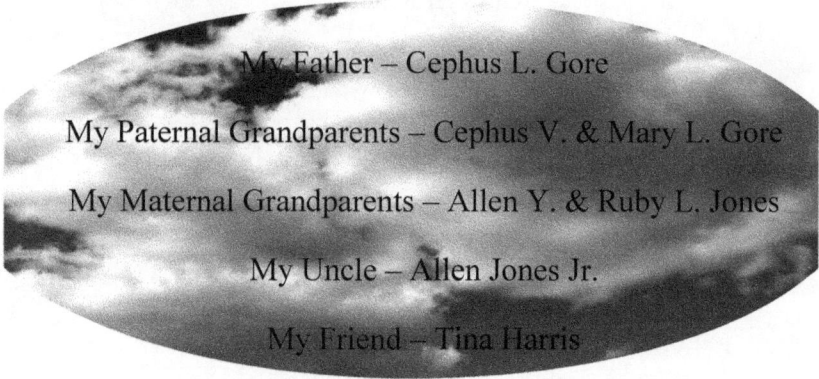

My Father – Cephus L. Gore

My Paternal Grandparents – Cephus V. & Mary L. Gore

My Maternal Grandparents – Allen Y. & Ruby L. Jones

My Uncle – Allen Jones Jr.

My Friend – Tina Harris

You make up my "great cloud of witnesses".

Hebrews 12:1 {AMP}
12 Therefore, since we are surrounded by so great a cloud of witnesses [who by faith have testified to the truth of God's absolute faithfulness], stripping off every unnecessary weight and the sin which so easily *and* cleverly entangles us, let us run with endurance *and* active persistence the race that is set before us,

TABLE OF CONTENTS

John 3:30 (NKJV)
³⁰ He must increase, but I *must* decrease.

John the Baptist

"This nation must decrease and Israel must increase."
Rev. Christopher Gore

INTRODUCTION
Moving Past the Election of 2016!

Well, here we are. The 2016 election cycle is over and we have a new president, Donald J. Trump. You may have voted for Hillary, Gary, Evan, Jill, Donald, or you may have chosen to not vote at all. Despite what your choice was, we all must deal with what has happened. This election is over. We all must move on from here.

I voted for Donald. I am glad that he won but I was completely shocked by his win. I was shocked because I feared that the naïve electorate of this nation. I feared they would push Hillary into office despite her open hatred for this country, our values, and our way of life. We have been assaulted with a constant barrage of misinformation, misdirection and straight-up lies from the political elites on both the Democratic and Republican sides of our political system.

The antichrist spirit has been working overtime through these elites since the inauguration of former President Barack. These elites have been actively working to further the agenda of the evil one, satan, for this country. It seemed an impossible mission to defeat the power-filled machine that was behind Hillary. Hillary's machine was driven by strong principalities and powers. These principalities and powers are still at work and we are not out of danger.

I am glad that Donald won but I am more concerned about the people of this nation who are still blinded by the principalities and powers' that are still behind Barack and Hillary. There are masses of minions who have blindly followed them everywhere and have overlooked all the evil that they have done. If Hillary would have won this election she would have continued to advance the antichrist agenda and opened a bigger door for the jezebel/ahab spirit to push this nation farther into darkness.

Through Donald this nation has been granted an extension of God's grace. We must not waste this opportunity. We must seize the day and advance the Kingdom of Heaven. Donald is a picture of King David in the Bible. David was a man after God's own heart. He loved the Lord and he wasn't asking to be King. He was just minding his own business and the Lord chose him. God brought Donald forth for such a time as this to give the United States another chance to serve Him.

There is a "greater works" for this nation to accomplish and because God's people interceded God opened the door for His King David to come forth. It's not an accident that Donald became our President. It is the divine will of the Almighty God. It is His will that is being done not mans. It is His will that is being done not the Democratic or Republican Party's elites. You cannot stop what God is going to do. The stage has been set and no one can upstage God.

My purpose for writing this book is to bring light to these simple truths. God has been, is, and always will be in control of the destiny of this nation and the nation of Israel not the elites. You can doubt this if you want but there is no one like God. God knows and sees all the things that are going on within our government. These things have not escaped His watchful eye.

God does care about the things that go on within our nation. Even though the antichrist spirit has made great strides and inroads into our government God has made a way for His promises to come to pass to His remnant. My hope is that this book will allow you to see and know that God has not left us.

Selah

1

PATTERNED AFTER DESTRUCTION
Noah, Elijah, King Saul, & King David...

2 Peter 2: 1 – 8 {Amplified}
1BUT ALSO [in those days] there arose **false prophets among the people, just as there will be false teachers among yourselves,** who will subtly and stealthily introduce heretical doctrines (destructive heresies), even **denying and disowning** the Master Who bought them, **bringing upon themselves swift destruction. 2**And many will follow their immoral ways and lascivious doings; because of them the True Way will be maligned and defamed. **3**And in their covetousness (lust, greed) they will exploit you with false (cunning) arguments. From of old the sentence [of condemnation] for them has not been idle; their destruction (eternal misery) has not been asleep. **4**For God did not [even] spare angels that sinned, but cast them

into hell, delivering them to be kept there in pits of gloom till the judgment and their doom.

5And He spared not the ancient world, but preserved Noah, a preacher of righteousness, with seven other persons, when He brought a flood upon the world of ungodly [people]. 6And He condemned to ruin and extinction the cities of Sodom and Gomorrah, reducing them to ashes [and thus] set them forth as an example to those who would be ungodly; 7And He rescued righteous Lot, greatly worn out and distressed by the wanton ways of the ungodly and lawless-- 8For that just man, living [there] among them, tortured his righteous soul every day with what he saw and heard of [their] unlawful and wicked deeds--

We are living in the last days. In this season, the false teachers and prophets are doing there "God ordained" thing but the Lord wants you to see the deception that these false teachers and prophets are walking in. The Church does not begin to understand the season that we are now living is a season of judgment by our own making. The question upon everyone's minds that is begging to be answered the most... is what is really about to happen?

What I have observed through studying Bible history is that there are times when the world will fall into patterns. Some of these patterns are positive and some are negative. There are many patterns that are going on at this given season but there are three that I want to highlight. They are the patterns that follow the Days of Noah, the patterns that follow the Days of Elijah, and the patterns that follow king Saul versus king David.

We can see from Biblical history that these patterns bring with them certain spiritual conflicts. These conflicts first began in the spirit realm and are later felt in the natural realm. Some may feel or be aware of these conflicts because they can be spiritually discerned by those who are walking in the Spirit. These conflicts are fought by real spiritual beings. These beings are both good and evil. The good beings or angels fight at God's command and on His behalf. The bad beings or demonic angels fight at the devil's command and on the devil's behalf.

Because we are in these patterns we can examine what is going on in the spiritual atmosphere and tie it directly to demon groupings that have been sent to hinder the plan of God. If we can learn the history of what took place in the Bible, find the pattern and do the exact opposite of that pattern herein our time we may be able to break the cycles of sin and iniquity that are attached to these patterns. When we break the cycle of sin and iniquity we can stop the forces of hell from gaining a foothold and stronghold over our nation

The principalities and powers operating during these seasons are getting stronger because of sin. Because sin is growing and has grown we are feeling the same pressure that Noah and Elijah felt in the Bible days. This sin brought a season of great spiritual darkness similar in nature and in intensity to what was experienced in the Bible during the Days of Noah and the Days of Elijah. The jezebel/ahab spirit, the antichrist spirit, and many other spirits that rule and reign with these have been unleashed in greater levels due to the increase of sin in the spiritual atmosphere

We have been in a dual pattern that is related to the Days of Noah and the Days of Elijah. The pattern of the Days of Noah can be evidenced through the growth of sin viewed through man's inhumanities to man. We find this evidenced by the darkness becoming so dark that people are committing the most heinous acts such as cannibalism and necromancy. These practices once thought to be taboo and limited to third world countries are now on the rise as the darkness in this earth has grown darker. More and more news reports reveal that now people in first world countries are partaking of these levels of depravity.

The Days of Elijah can be evidenced through the manifestation of power struggles via the Church and governments of this world. Elijah was always fighting against the sin-filled government leaders. The power that is in the anointing will come against any governmental leadership that is not godly. We need the Elijah's to come forth and be used by God to voice His opposition to sin. It's exciting to know that there are Godly politicians and government officials in this nation but there are others who are not and God is raising up Elijah's to confront them and have them receive the chastening of the Lord.

In the days of Noah and the days of Elijah it was not uncommon to see greater concentrations and strengths of the jezebel/ahab spirit in manifestation. It was not uncommon to see greater concentrations of the antichrist spirit. These spirits contain wickedness and sin which are not limited to but can include: sexual perversion, mental perversion, licentiousness, and effeminate spirits. These spirits also manifested themselves in people through greed, debauchery, extreme hatred, and uncleanness of all types.

There are no new sins. The same sins that we are battling today have been around for centuries. So, when man entertains these sin patterns doorways and even gateways open for the demons to act out these past conflicts that were seen in Biblical times. So, when I say that we are in a pattern that is similar to the Days of Noah and Days of Elijah, I am not saying that Noah and Elijah have come back from the dead and are walking around on the earth. I am saying that the same sin natures that were alive and prevalent during those time periods can be found to be alive and prevalent in our time.

Sin doesn't just affect us as a people sin destroys the spiritual atmosphere. Because sin grows in concentration it affects our entire nation and world. It affects everything on this planet. Sin is what is contributing to the increase in natural weather phenomenon. In this nation alone we have seen an increase in hurricanes, tornadoes, and violent thunderstorms. Around the world, there have been tsunamis, earthquakes, typhoons, cyclones and ice storms. These are all directly related to the unatoned sin that lies in the atmosphere and the crust of the earth. It's not global warming or climate change, it's the sins of the people on the earth causing the earth to react and respond.

It's this concentration of sin that contributes to the spiritual climate of our nation. The battle that we just saw manifested in the natural via the 2016 election cycle took place in the spiritual realm first. Our election showed a true battle between light and darkness. This election cycle brought the worst out of some and the best out of others in the Church and out. This was due to the many false teachers and prophets working in the Church. The refusal by leaders in the Church to walk in holiness has caused the power to be drained from the Church. The Church needs more Elijah's to fight against and confront the sin that is manifested via these false teachers and prophets who blur the lines of truth from the people. The main truth being, "Be ye holy, for I am Holy."

All it takes is one person to say no to sin. That one person through the obedience of repenting of the sin and staying free from it can open the door for God's heart to be moved and our nation changed from the inside out. One person can change the spiritual atmosphere in a region and remove the links that would connect that region to sin. The atmosphere that we feel and live in is directly related to the principalities and powers that are prevalent during these seasons.

The final pattern that I want to discuss is the pattern of king Saul versus king David. This pattern can be evidence through looking at former President Barack and our current President Donald. Barack will constitute a type related to king Saul and Donald will constitute a type related to king David. Barack has a strong islamic heritage which disqualifies him from being a part of the actual lineage of king Saul. However, when you look at the behaviors king Saul and Barack had they are similar in nature.

King Saul was a man of the people. He was popular in his own right and the people loved him until king David came along. King Saul had a fundamental character flaw that kept him from being a man that God could trust. King Saul loved to obey the voice of the people more than the voice of God.

If you look at Barack's administration it was instrumental in paving the way for a pro-islamic agenda to infiltrate and take over various branches of our government. Ever since 9-11 this pro-islamic agenda has been growing within our nation. As this nation has been moved away from Christianity towards a many religions mindset it is far more difficult to criticize those who are pro-islamic. Their reach has gone deep into our culture and political system as well.

Prophetically speaking we are in a time of judgment that is unprecedented. The sins of the people have come up before the Father just like Abel's blood cried out from the ground. Enoch said that the voice of Abel's spirit who was slain by Cain his brother accused Cain, until his seed be destroyed before the face of the earth; until his seed perish from the seed of the human race.[1] What Enoch was relating to us is that until there is a full payment for the sin the blood of the person sinned against will cry out in the courts of heaven. The Church does not understand this and neither does this nation.

God's laws have not changed. There are over 58, 586, 256 babies aborted since Roe versus Wade in 1973 and if Abel's blood is still crying out from over 6, 000 years ago how much more is the blood of those babies crying out?[2] The sins of the people of our nation are many. I don't need to list them, you know what they are. The Church has only atoned for this on a surface level. The only reason that the Church has done minimal atonement is

---

[1] The Book of Enoch - Laurence, Richard; 1883
[2] http://www.lifenews.com/2016/01/14/58586256-abortions-in-america-since-roe-v-wade-in-1973/

because the Church has many things in common with the world. If you look at the Church, then you see the world. There is no distinction between the two. The Church in the name of being open to everyone has married itself to the world.

> **Deuteronomy 8:19 {NKJV}**
> [19] Then it shall be, if you by any means forget the LORD your God, and follow other gods, and serve them and worship them, I testify against you this day that you shall surely perish.

You cannot mate (fornicate) with the gods of this world and serve the one, true living God. It will not work. It will stir Him to jealousy. We really don't want to be on the wrong side of His jealousy.

> **Exodus 20:5 {NKJV}**
> [5] you shall not bow down to them nor serve them. For I, the LORD your God, *am* a jealous God, visiting the iniquity of the fathers upon the children to the third and fourth *generations* of those who hate Me

> **Exodus 34:14 {NKJV}**
> [14] (for you shall worship no other god, for the LORD, whose name *is* Jealous, *is* a jealous God),

> **Deuteronomy 4:24 {NKJV}**
> [24] For the LORD your God *is* a consuming fire, a jealous God.

> **Deuteronomy 6:15 {NKJV}**
> [15] (for the LORD your God *is* a jealous God among you), lest the anger of the LORD your God be aroused

against you and destroy you from the face of the earth.

We know this but God demands our single-hearted devotion to Him. He does not intend to share our attention with another god, (Anything that we put in the place that God is supposed to be in). This is the God whom we serve. This is a part of His nature, jealous means to be red; God becomes red when His people violate His laws, His ways. When God's children refuse to follow what He has asked them to do, it stirs His jealousy, His redness. You can provoke God's jealousy to spring forth upon you.

Because of the sins of this nation we have caused God's heart to break and weep over us. This nation was founded on a covenant with God. It was founded on the belief that He is the Supreme Creator of all. Through time and many evil people the truth of our history has been changed and corrupted to the degree that even now our former President made the following statement, "Islam has been woven into the fabric of our country since its founding."[3] This is not the truth. This nation was founded on Christian values.

This twisting of the truth about our nation's Godly heritage has given many reason to pause. This has opened the door for deep perversion to come in. This deep perversion sets this nation as the recipient of God's wrath.

---

[3] http://www.cnsnews.com/news/article/susan-jones/obama-islam-has-been-woven-fabric-our-country-its-founding

Genesis 6:1-6 {NKJV}
6 Now it came to pass, when men began to multiply on the face of the earth, and daughters were born to them, ² that the sons of God saw the daughters of men, that they *were* beautiful; and they took wives for themselves of all whom they chose.
³ And the LORD said, "My Spirit shall not strive with man forever, for he *is* indeed flesh; yet his days shall be one hundred and twenty years."⁴ There were giants on the earth in those days, and also afterward, when the sons of God came in to the daughters of men and they bore *children* to them. Those *were* the mighty men who *were* of old, men of renown.
⁵ Then the LORD saw that the wickedness of man *was* great in the earth, and *that* every intent of the thoughts of his heart *was* only evil continually. ⁶ And the LORD was sorry that He had made man on the earth, and He was grieved in His heart.

Our God is crying. He is crying over the lack of commitment, the lack of love, the lack of truth that is being demonstrated to the world by His Church. Jesus laid His life down for us so that we could have life more abundantly. Sin and the degradation thereof does not give us life more abundantly. Our sin is causing God to cry and mourn over what he would like to give us but can't. Sin is causing God to cry over the men, women, and children who are everyday walking a path of destruction that leads them into Hell and away from God.

When you look at **verse 5**, you can understand the reason for God crying. The wickedness of men grew. It grew to such a state that every evil desire that man decided to fulfill was accomplished. His plan, His desire was for us to love one another and treat each other well. Because of sin and the corruption that it brings it leads us to self-destruction. It births and creates desires that will drive them to commit sins so heinous and so despicable that it will move God to react. Deep in the heart people have risen to a place where they think they do not need God.

Many prophets have been saying that the Church is in a transition period. I agree but do we understand what this transition is all about. Our western mindset has us blind in some respects to what God is doing. This is a season of retribution for the sins of the Church and the beginning of the end of the Gentile Dispensation. I believe with everything within me that God is transitioning the world stage back to the Middle East, back to the land of His beloved nation Israel. And just like John the Baptist we (the West) must decrease.

Unfortunately for us, this decrease is going to be meted out in some severe judgments from God towards the Church in America. God is transitioning at this given time and He is moving the focal point from the Gentiles to the Jews. I am not pretending to know the whole picture but I believe if you take a step back you will see that some things are odd about this current election cycle. In studying scripture, there is one pattern that I have found with consistency, and that is when God judges a nation, He raises up a heathen nation to enact that punishment upon the nation that He is judging. This happened all the time to Israel. So it is not a stretch of the imagination to see what God is going to be doing as He judges us. I believe that God is using Russia to do this.

There are many who have a political agenda, even those in the Church, and that agenda goes contrary to the plan of God. That plan is the transitioning of the world's focus from this nation back to Israel. Only God knows all that He is doing in this hour and it would behoove us to stay close to His heart so that we can fully know what to say to His people. I have had a strong sense of alarm since the beginning of former President George W. Bush's administration. His eight years in office was a time of plenty for the United States. It was a time that those who were discerning were storing up and preparing for the harsh times that we as the Church knew were ahead of us.

The major warning the prophets issued was to get out of debt. The prophets warned that personal debt and national debt would rise and if we were not watchful we could be trapped in the system because of debt. Many prophets predicted the fall of our nations dollar and monetary system. They predicted a major crash of the stock market. This has not happened yet but many secular financial analysts believe that this fall is still yet to come. There have been mini crashes and mini periods of recession but we are still headed for another big depression. This depression will once again affect the entire world.

There were some who heeded the warnings that came from the true prophets. The season of prosperity that was brought on by former President George W. Bush came to an end. All of the signs are here and all of the experts know that a major transition is going to occur in our economy. God gave the Church prophets with warnings but the Church spit upon them and made them of no account. They downplayed any message that they gave and discredited them at every chance they could. There is so much sorrow headed our way and the American Church is not prepared for the destruction that is coming to us.

Many in our nation are living paycheck to paycheck. There is more poverty now than ever before. There is more debt than ever before and the sad part is that many in our nation are completely oblivious to this. **As of December 2016 the nations of Japan and China hold approximately 35.8 % of the national debt.** [4]

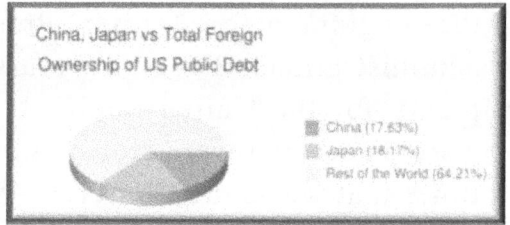

China, Japan vs Total Foreign Ownership of US Public Debt

China (17.63%)
Japan (18.17%)
Rest of the World (64.21%)

The national debt clock continues to tick higher and higher. **At the time of this book the national debt is calculated as being in the neighborhood of 19.8 trillion dollars. Let's break this down in every day terms. If you spent $1 million a day since Jesus was born, you would have not spent $1 trillion by now...** [5] That is an astounding figure. This nation is vulnerable in so many ways.

This nation is being judged. Whether you want to accept this or not the Church has already started being judged for the things that it (the Church) is not. God in His grace has given us so much time to repent and prepare for the days that are now upon us but because of the corruption in the leadership of the Church the message has been diluted and in some cases even shut off. But God in His mercy has allowed a few faithful voices to remain and

[4] http://www.davemanuel.com/us-national-debt-clock.php Dave Manuel
[5] http://demonocracy.info/infographics/usa/us_debt/us_debt.html

sound the trumpet and those who had an ear have heard what thus saith the Lord.

I must say that based upon some older prophecies that I have read and studied by some older prophets who are still not popular with today's church leadership, this nation is entering into its time of judgment. Say what you will about it, deny it if it makes you feel good, but the truth will stand throughout all of eternity. There has been a lot of truth come out recently and the leadership in the Church has not liked that truth. It didn't fit with their agenda but I have learned that the only agenda that is important and lasting is God's agenda.

> **Jeremiah 25:29 {NKJV}**
> [29] For behold, I begin to bring calamity on the city which is called by My name, and should you be utterly unpunished? You shall not be unpunished, for I will call for a sword on all the inhabitants of the earth," says the LORD of hosts.'

There is no doubt in my mind that God has called our nation to greatness. I believe that Donald is a major part of this. There is no doubt in my mind that we were a nation who answered God's call. As long as we are following the precepts and commands of God our nation will be OK.

However, we must acknowledge the truth that this nation has been on a downward spiral for eight years or more. The infrastructure that was put in place by Barack was strategic. It was purposeful and deliberate. The antichrist spirit embedded itself within our nation and the fact has to be pointed out that the Church and leadership in the Church turned its eye in the name of tolerance to the corruption. The decline in holiness in the leadership in the Church spread like poison throughout our nation.

When you tie this together with the enemy moving through the atheist movement, witchcraft, and the growth of the church of satan the saltiness of the Church has been decimated over the last eight years. Looking at the big picture, the promises of "Hope" and "Change" were just the candy that was needed to lead the unchurched in this nation straight over the cliff right into Hell.

It didn't take much to draw masses of people in this nation into the arms of the antichrist spirit. This spirit along with a spirit of deception was coupled with strong delusion and many gave in to the lies and believed everything this spirit told them to do. Right down to killing their children. It was all done in the name of freedom and convenience. Many have sold their soul for a life of ease and comfort. Many are addicted to alcohol, drugs, entertainment, sex, and television.

Many in this state are only concerned about prosperity and anyone who promises prosperity will gain a steady following. This nation achieved prosperity because we were once godly. God blessed us and gave to us because of our holiness. We stopped being holy as a nation but the prosperity appeared to continue for a season. We failed to realize a deception that may come from prosperity. That is the deception that allows a person to be deluded into believing they are spiritually OK. If you continue down this path, God will leave you and eventually your blessings will dwindle away. Sometimes it takes a while for the blessings to dwindle down. The prosperity doesn't stop right away. When this happens, people take this as a sign that they are still alright with God. They are not.

2

I'M SORRY
Where Our Nation Really Is...

I know that there is dispute over this passage of scripture but the Bible says the gifts of God are without repentance. Prosperity is a gift that has come to this nation and whether you know this or not, you can be prosperous and be in sin. Look at the amount of rich people who are sin laden; countless movie stars and rock stars who live a life of lewdness yet they continue to prosper financially. The sickness that can come with being blessed is that you can automatically think that you are all right. You think that you are fine because of your prosperity. The same curse has befallen this nation because we are prosperous we assume that we are alright with God and we are not.

> **Revelation 3:17-19 {NKJV}**
> [17] Because you say, 'I am rich, have become wealthy, and have need of nothing'—and do not know that you are wretched, miserable,

> poor, blind, and naked— [18] I counsel you to
> buy from Me gold refined in the fire, that you
> may be rich; and white garments, that you may
> be clothed, *that* the shame of your nakedness
> may not be revealed; and anoint your eyes
> with eye salve, that you may see. [19] As many
> as I love, I rebuke and chasten. Therefore be
> zealous and repent.

The American dream is to be rich enough to do
whatever you want whenever you want. For many this
dream has turned into a fantasy world that includes living
above your means. The availability of personal credit and
credit worthiness has lured many into repetitive cycles of
sin. Covetousness abounds because there is discontent
with what one has. There is a continual striving for more
and the desire to gain more becomes insatiable. The more
things that you want, the more time it takes to acquire them
which takes more time away from God and your family.
We have lost our children because we are so busy trying to
give them more. This more is what really is hurting them
but we have taught them they need to feel and be like
everyone else. In all of this many will lose their salvation
and we will eventually lose this nation.

This passage in **Revelation 3: 17 to 18** is the
passage that is written to the Laodicean Church, a.k.a. the
lukewarm church. God spewed them out of His mouth
because they said that they had need of nothing. How
many times have we heard people say, "I am fine, I don't
need anybody, or anything?" Dangerous words for the
dangerous times that our nations is in. This is all because
of the abundance that we are blessed with. This is an
opening that the antichrist spirit used to his advantage.

There has been a consistent and persistent attack by the antichrist spirit through Barack Obama and those who follow him. These attacks caused many to lose hope for any real change in our government. This lack of hope minimized the possibility that the tide of sin and degradation that prevailed over the last eight years would ever stop churning. That churning has produced a wake of spiritual disasters that we still have not fully accounted for in the spirit realm.

Barack & Hillary represent a sect of people in our society who believe that they are entitled to everything. Nothing is earned. It is to be given. Whenever this sect makes a demand they expect that the government or someone is just going to give them what they have demanded. Whether it is a house or car or food, the expectation is that someone else is going to provide these items for them. It doesn't matter what it costs the person providing the items, it only matters that the items are given to the demander of the item. Our society has fundamentally changed from a society of givers to a society of takers.

Hillary was on course to continue what Barack had started. Like Barack she was going to advance an agenda that supported and promoted the antichrist spirit. Barack had a severe hatred for Christianity and the Nation of Israel. We saw the advancement of political correctness and a straight forward attack on Christian values take place via Barack. A Hillary administration would have continued this advancement and this would directly lead to the destruction and demolition of this nation.

In the 2008 election, the people chose Obama to be their king. They chose him for one simple reason. He promised them everything that they ever wanted. They did not have to work or do anything to earn it. History has proven that nations who have more people living off the government fail. It is not sustainable for over half of your citizens to sit at home and collect a check for doing nothing. The nations that have done that have all collapsed under their own weight. When a nation and its leaders encourage this type of behavior it breeds an atmosphere for corruption.

I am not a conspiracy theorist. I just read my Bible. I know what I have seen and have read and come to know as the truth. You have to read the parts of the Bible that people don't like to read. The genealogies, those little stories where people were killed, they were judged for the things that they did, those stories that had horror and tragedy in them. It's in these stories that you begin to see all sides of our God. I don't have a slanted opinion of God. I don't only believe that He is a God of love, I also believe through reading His word, faith comes by hearing and hearing by the Word of God, that God is a God of wrath.

I have read David's stories where God became angry at David's sin and God sent His wrath and judged the people, because of one man's sin. I have read how God in His wrath caused the earth to open up and swallow Korah and his followers up into the earth because of their rebellion. It's in the Word. Does God's Word lie? It does not! I have faith that not one jot or tittle of this Word will pass away until all of it is fulfilled. **(Matt 5: 18)**

Stay in the dark if you choose too but I believe deep in my heart that there is something going on that is so much bigger and darker than we can even fathom. There are things that are lining up in this nation that are ugly and need a complete change.

Let me burst your bubble the Church is still on a downward spiral. Christians are not having Children by birth or adoption. Church attendance is down, church growth is down, average Bible knowledge is said to be on a 5th grade level, tithing is down, and volunteer workers are down. It's was quoted by Perry Stone that ten percent of the people who attend church do all of the work in the church. Compare this to the amount of growth in the Muslim community.

Muslims are having 12 to 15 children per family. Their attendance in their mosques is up. You don't go to Mosque and not participate. Men go to Muslim churches. When was the last time you seen a group of men come to church on their own. Not so in this nation, but Muslim men go to church without their wives. That says a lot. This was in the Jerusalem Post on Aug 28, 2008, **"The Russian-backed Chechen President Ramzan Kadyrov will inaugurate the "largest mosque in Europe" on October 17 in Chechnya, the Russian official news agency Novosty reported. Over 10,000 worshipers will be able to pray inside the mosque,"**

We can't get people to come to church on a consistent basis but the Muslims can. Will the Church of this nation be honest and admit that its members are not really into serving Christ? No! And because of this the Church is in trouble. There is no leadership in the church today and this plague is increasing.

1 Peter 4:17 {NKJV}
[17] For the time *has come* for judgment to begin at the house of God; and if *it begins* with us first, what will *be* the end of those who do not obey the gospel of God?

It's scary but true. Judgment has begun in God's house. All across this nation the Church has been judged for the lack of holiness in the leadership in these days of darkness. The church was supposed to be speaking on behalf of God yet it continues to speak on behalf of the many idols that are alive and well in the American culture. If you check your Bible God didn't mind so much when the ordinary people sinned but when the priesthood became corrupt that's when judgment really fell on the children of Israel.

1 Samuel 2:25 {NKJV}
[25] If one man sins against another, God will judge him. But if a man sins against the LORD, who will intercede for him?" Nevertheless they did not heed the voice of their father, because the LORD desired to kill them.

These were Eli's words when he tried to tell his sons (they were priests) to stop sinning against God. I don't have to tell you how corrupt the church has become. You know it already. Many leaders standing behind pulpits today are living on borrowed time. They have unrepentant sins in their hearts and they have assumed that because their gifting worked that God still accepted them just like they were. Think about this Hophni and Phineas were still performing sacrifices and atoning for the sins of the people while they themselves were not right with God. The anointing didn't stop flowing but all the while they were storing up the wrath of God for themselves.

The top leaders in the church today did seek the face of God concerning this election but because they went before God with a preconceived idea of what He was doing in this hour, they did not have the ability to see what God is doing. Because they walked in Eli's blindness they were not able to see the truth. The Leaders in the Church don't want to accept this thing but God's agenda at times brings judgment to the people He loves.

Because God has a plan for this country, He put it on the heart of the Remnant to cry out and repent for this nation. God heard the cry of the Remnant. He saw how our freedoms were being taken from us. He saw how we as a nation were oppressing the nation of Israel and not blessing them. He saw how we are really oppressing our poor. He saw how we are becoming Godless and hedonistic. He stepped in and made a way for this nation to turn around.

The devil has his hand deep in this country. The devil is seeking to devour anyone who gets in his way. I like many others have been concerned for a long time with the spiritual condition of the Church. There are those within the walls of the Church who just want to party, they don't want to get their hands dirty and follow the ways of righteousness. They don't want to stand and fight against the forces of darkness that are growing in power every day. There is a mentality of compromise that has grown into the Church that needs to be removed.

There are those who are actively fighting this compromise and the forces of darkness that work with it. They are in this battle for the Lord. They stand and fight day in and day out. They are trying to get the truth to God's people. None of them delights in being the bearer of bad news but like the Jeremiah's of old; they stand and deliver the bitter scroll. It tastes bad but it's going to stir God's Church to change. This is not a truth that is easy to administer.

When you look at the atmosphere in the Church it is spiritually dark. The Church is walking in strong deception. We need the Spirit of God to give us discernment like never before so we can guide the people into Christ's light.

I'm sorry but you must know the truth. You must know that this scripture is coming to pass in this nation and those who hate God will not prevail. Peter was clear in his admonition to the Church. False prophets and false teachers will be among us. They will lead many good people astray and cause them to walk in darkness and that is sin. I'm sorry but no matter what you believe the Bible remains true. You cannot be deceived by the false prophets and the false teachers. The destruction they bring will cause righteous people to be vexed like Lot.

For those who feel like Lot felt, vexed by the sin and degradation around you, God wants you to hold on. Keep yourself separate from the world because Jesus Christ is returning for you in a time and season that you know not of. Moreover, we have to stand and tell the Church to take in these bitter scrolls so that the Church can be cleansed from all unrighteousness.

Some in the Body of Christ don't like for the Remnant to talk about this but the truth is the truth. This election cycle is the biggest sign of how dark our country and its leaders have become. There is a day of repayment for the things that have been done in the dark. We cannot put our hope in our political system to rescue us. Our hope must be in Jesus Christ. Our hope must be in the Father who knows all that He is doing in this hour.

> **John 16:12 {NKJV}**
> [12] "I still have many things to say to you, but you cannot bear *them* now.

Jesus was tempted in all points and in all ways like we are. This even included frustration. Being a prophetic person there are things that God will share with me that are timed. They can only be shared at a later date. This is cool because God has intimacy with us as His children and that intimacy produces knowledge of future events and circumstances that are going on in our world. I am sorry but this country is not where it should be with God. I am sorry but there are things going on behind the scenes in the way of sin still that need to be addressed. They have been improperly repented of and because of this bowls of wrath have been accumulating for this nation.

Do not be fooled, God will not be mocked. Just because Donald is our president that does not mean that we get a free pass for our sins. You can see this evidenced by how much Donald is having to fight with the press, the leaders in the Democratic party, the Republican elites, the die-hard fans of Barack, and the staunch supporters of Hillary. Our nation is headed for destruction.

3

A HOUSE DIVIDED AGAINST ITSELF
Exposing the Agendas in the Church!

> **Mark 3:22-25 {NKJV}**
> 22 And the scribes who came down from Jerusalem said, "He has Beelzebub," and, "By the ruler of the demons He casts out demons." 23 So He called them to *Himself* and said to them in parables: "How can Satan cast out Satan? 24 If a kingdom is divided against itself, that kingdom cannot stand. 25 And if a house is divided against itself, that house cannot stand.

You would think that the Church would learn something from the enemy. The enemy no matter what closes ranks in with each other and they fight their collective enemy together as one hand. The Church in this nation has not done this. The Church in this nation continues to go off of many different agendas. There is a vision but it is multiplied and to the degree that we as the Church cannot get on the same page with each other is the degree to which the enemy can run over us. The Church has lost elections since the

Bill Clinton because the Church had so many different visions that the people got confused and had no one in which to turn.

If you ask any ten people in the Church what their views are on politics you will get that many answers. The Church has done a terrible job in this regard. You should always vote. You should always vote Christian values. The problem comes in when those in the Church no longer know what Christian values are. The elections of 2008 and 2012 were significant because they have proven that Christians opted not to vote.

> **Over 62 million voters cast their ballot for George W. Bush in 2004. Less than 60 million voters cast their ballot for John McCain in 2008. And somewhere under 57-59 Million voters cast their ballot for Mitt Romney in 2012.** [6]

This is a difference of approximately 3 million people. The Christians did not have a clear voice and many opted to refrain from voting. We don't know what would have happened in the 2008 and 2012 elections if those people would have made it to the polls. What is clear is that we are giving up our power by not participating in the system that was set up for us. There are many who chose to stay home during this election cycle because of the confusing messages coming from leadership in the Church in 2016.

We were supposed to be on the same team. We were supposed to be working and flowing in the Spirit yet there were so many different opinions as to what should be done. It should not be

---

[6] http://www.redstate.com/diary/griffinelection/2012/11/14/what-went-wrong-in-2012-the-case-of-the-4-million-missing-voters/

this hard for leadership to encourage the people to do the right thing. It should not be hard for us as a people to stand up for what's right and moral and Godly but it is. The line had been muddied. No one was willing to stand for good they would much rather be silent than to make a stand for what is right.

The leaders in the Church have a part to play in this. Sometimes it can be very frustrating listening to prophetic people. They intentionally talk in riddles and each one has a subjective meaning. This year several prophecies came out in regards to the election. If you were for Donald or Hillary you could interpret that either one would win. Prophets are human and they are subject to the same tendencies and pitfalls as preachers. Sometimes they get diarrhea of the mouth. This is not a time to be popular but a time to be in the Spirit. There are many who are in prophetic circles that were making bold proclamations about how God is bringing prosperity to the United States. This seems contradictory to the patterns of righteousness that God has established.

The Church has to learn to not give a mixed message.

> **"It's not the personality, where we vote for the personality," he added. "In the words of [Covenant Church Founding Pastor] Michael Hayes, that's idolatry."**[7]
>
> **Hispanic evangelical leader Rev. Samuel Rodriguez is urging Christians to vote on "platform and principle" and not "personality" — appearing to give a nod to**

---

[7] https://nhclc.org/2016-election/rev-samuel-rodriguez-urges-christians-to-vote-on-platform-principle

GOP nominee Donald Trump, The Christian Post **reported.**[8]

Mike Jacobs declared that as he and Cindy travel abroad, they are constantly having to repent to their fellow Christians "for actions taken by the leadership of the United States of America" in pushing homosexuality upon other nations.[9]

"I'm a pastor. I don't endorse candidates or place bumper stickers on my car. But I am protective of the Christian faith. If a public personality calls on Christ one day and calls someone a "bimbo" the next, is something not awry? And to do so, not once, but repeatedly? Unrepentantly? Unapologetically? Can we not expect a tone that would set a good example for our children? We stand against bullying in schools. Shouldn't we do the same in presidential politics?" Says Max Lucado[10]

Beth Moore wasn't alone in her condemnation of Trump. Her comments sent ripples around the evangelical world and were seconded by Christian mega-speaker and author Christine Caine."[11]

So who do you vote for? What basis do you make your decisions off of? All of these leaders have good reasons for believing what they believed but what is the

---

[8] https://nhclc.org/2016-election/rev-samuel-rodriguez-urges-christians-to-vote-on-platform-principle
[9] http://www.rightwingwatch.org/post/cindy-jacobs-christians-must-vote-to-stop-the-us-from-polluting-other-nations-with-gay-pride-flags/
[10] http://religionnews.com/2016/06/21/7-conservative-christians-who-are-not-supporting-trump/
[11] http://www.thedailybeast.com/articles/2016/10/10/beth-moore-the-christian-women-speaking-out-about-trump-s-bad-news.html

right choice? The God choice. If you talk to different people each and every time you will get a different answer. This is sad but true. We cannot stand because we are not one. We cannot stand against the darkness because we don't understand what that darkness is doing and has been doing for a very long time now.

The enemy is persistent. He has been working at destroying us from the very foundations of the world when he was removed by God from heaven. We have to know what is on the mind and heart of God to even understand what He is saying in this hour. There were millions of Christians who wanted to do the right thing and vote the right way but the truth of the matter is that it didn't just start with this Presidential Election. It started with the Elections on your local level. We need to begin to teach people that the person who is running for the head of the school board, dog catcher, judge, these people and positions in government matter. They matter and the people occupying these offices need to be clean, moral, God-fearing people. But hindsight is nothing at this stage of the game. This should have been done years ago.

Now in the day and age of the internet we have blogs, YouTube, twitter and other media with which to stay in contact with people. We can send messages all over to the Body of Christ who is plugged in. Prophets like to send out these messages as well. This has its up and downs. In the right hands, these are powerful tools that can be used for God to get His voice out to the people but in the wrong hands it can bring a lot of confusion and even division. The devil had control of key people in the leadership of the Church. Anyone who is in leadership who has a sin nature is vulnerable to be taken over and used by the devil. The devil can use them to preach and speak his message at any time.

Because our teachings have been corrupted by man's wisdom, the Church is prone to error. Let me jump onto greasy grace for a moment. The biggest error message going right now in the Church is that God has given you grace to allow you to sin. This message is sending more people to Hell every day and the leaders in the Church who are promoting these teachings are responsible for those souls. God does give us grace but that Grace is so that we CHANGE. Grace is there for us to see God's love, know His heart and then be moved to Change. If you look at what Jesus did, He came to set the captives free and then He told them something else.

> **John 5:14 {NKJV}**
> [14] Afterward Jesus found him in the temple, and said to him, "See, you have been made well. Sin no more, lest a worse thing come upon you."

"Go and Sin no More!" That was a clear direct sign to stop doing what you are doing. Jesus told the man healed at the Pool of Bethesda to sin no more, lest a worse thing come upon you. That was not greasy grace. That was not I love you and I am gonna keep bad things from happening to you, that was a flat out get it together or you are really gonna be in trouble. This false doctrine is one of the more pervasive in the Church. It has wrapped itself around everything. For this election cycle, it was interesting to see how Donald went to the Church and professed his Christianity and everyone was happy. They did the same to Hillary. These statements satisfied some leaders in the Church and they were taken at face value.

There are two schools of thought going on in the church right now concerning politics and both of them are wrong. One school of thought is that the Church is not supposed to be involved in government/politics. I don't believe that this is scriptural because the King was always assigned a prophet that would speak into his life. David being a good example, had Samuel and Nathan. Ahab being a bad example had Elijah. So based upon that I don't really see how the Church is not supposed to be involved in government/politics.

The Second and more popular school of thought is that we are supposed to set up a government for Jesus Christ to come back to rule and reign in on this earth. The most obvious error about this teaching is that the Jesus Christ is coming back to this nation and is going to sit in the White House. Stop laughing, many Christians believe this error. This is so wrong. We American's have such a slanted vision of the Word of God. Jesus is not going to come back to this nation when He returns. When Jesus returns He will be returning to Jerusalem.

Some Christians believe that we the Christians are going to take over the government of this nation and rule and reign just like we are in heaven. This is a severe twisting of the teaching that is in the Bible that the Church is going to return to the earth and rule and reign with Christ for a thousand years. Where the people who teach this doctrine, miss is they leave out the part about the Christians being raptured out. They don't want to discuss that part they just want to come in and overthrow the government. I believe that it is this teaching that caused Christians to be placed on watch lists for groups as homegrown terrorists.

Let me burst another bubble. Jesus is coming back to be the King of the Jewish nation first. Remember when He was here the first time, the Jewish people were looking for a King to come in and overthrow their Roman oppressors. Clearing up these two errors will quickly cause a true believer to see that there is something wrong with the belief of us setting up a Kingdom for Jesus to return too. But let me go a little deeper with my quest to bring you the truth.

Jesus answered Pilate in **John 18: 36** with these words: **"My Kingdom is not of this world: if My kingdom were of this world, then would my servants fight that I should not be delivered to the Jews: but now is my kingdom not from hence.**

Seems rather simple to me, straight from Jesus' mouth, Jesus' kingdom is not of this world. Now this passage cross references to **Dan 2: 44** which I find very interesting. Let 's start with verse forty so that it makes sense.

> **Daniel 2:40-44 {NKJV}**
> [40] And the fourth kingdom shall be as strong as iron, in as much as iron breaks in pieces and shatters everything; and like iron that crushes, *that kingdom* will break in pieces and crush all the others. [41] Whereas you saw the feet and toes, partly of potter's clay and partly of iron, the kingdom shall be divided; yet the strength of the iron shall be in it, just as you saw the

> iron mixed with ceramic clay. [42] And *as* the toes of the feet *were* partly of iron and partly of clay, *so* the kingdom shall be partly strong and partly fragile. [43] As you saw iron mixed with ceramic clay, they will mingle with the seed of men; but they will not adhere to one another, just as iron does not mix with clay. [44] And in the days of these kings the God of heaven will set up a kingdom which shall never be destroyed; and the kingdom shall not be left to other people; it shall break in pieces and consume all these kingdoms, and it shall stand forever.

So, we can see here in this scripture that in the day that Jesus returns and God comes back and sets up a Kingdom there will be this fourth kingdom on the earth. It doesn't say that the Church will have a Kingdom established on the earth and Jesus will return and set up His Kingdom in that Kingdom. Read it again, so that you can see this clearly. Jesus is not coming to the earth to enter into that fourth Kingdom and take over.

Somehow someway Christians have taken this passage and tied it together with the false doctrine that we are to build a Kingdom for Christ to return to and they have come up with this idea that we need to overtake existing governments and set up our own government. Looking at the fourth kingdom in context with the first through the third kingdoms one can see that each of these four kingdoms was not operating with God. They were operating against God. Now, someone who has swallowed this false teaching down without studying all of the ins and outs of it will be deceived into this belief that we are to establish a government on this earth for Christ. **Verse 44** is very plain.

> **Daniel 2:44 {NKJV}**
> [44] And in the days of these kings the God of heaven will set up a kingdom which shall never be destroyed; and the kingdom shall not be left to other people; it shall break in pieces and consume all these kingdoms, and it shall stand forever.

That would lead me to believe that whatever Kingdom is set up and established on this earth will be destroyed by the kingdom that God is bringing to this earth when Christ returns. There is so much to consider in God's Word. If we are not working for God we are working against God. That is scripture. I want to point out one more thing in **Dan 2: 44.** The verse also says that this kingdom will not be left to other people, but it shall break in pieces and consume all of the existing kingdoms on the earth. It doesn't say that the Church's Kingdom will be left but it says that all, very important word, all will be consumed/destroyed.   The Church is moving down a dangerous path right now and more and more people are falling into this very strong delusion.

The times that we are living in are so serious. This election is a form of testing for this nation. We are being weighed in the balances and are being found wanting. We do not have our ears open and mindsets clear for the Lord to speak His wisdom into our hearts. We must drop our preconceived thoughts and allow God to speak to us exactly what it is that He is doing right now. The only way that we will hear the truth is that we first must acknowledge to God that we don't have a clue as to what He is doing. It is only as we express our weaknesses and blindness's as to what is really going on that God will allow us to see and hear what He is doing.

Who is so blind but the servant of the Lord? Who is so blind but the Church right now? Have you noticed something about prophetic people? Most of them have the sawed off shotgun approach. They just prophesy about everything. A sawed off shot gun has a wide spray from the shell fragments. It's not pinpoint accurate. The bullet brakes up into many pieces and goes all over the place. A rifle has one bullet and it hits the target in one place.

The prophets must stop this. If you are not hearing anything, just be honest and say I am not hearing anything. If you are wrong, be honest and say that you are wrong. We have too many shotgun prophets in the body adding more and more confusion to the mess that we already have going on. Take some advice, sit down and keep your mouth shut so you will not be labeled a self-appointed prophet or even a false prophet. Being labeled this way can destroy your credibility in the prophetic.

4

2016 ELECTION CYCLE
Sorting Through the Agendas in the Church!

This election has everyone saying everything and who really has heard the truth? Very few! Many are being deceived because they refuse to let go of what religious tradition has taught them even if it is wrong. We must become willing to accept and process the scripture as God sees it. Not as we see it, but as God sees it.

We cannot rely upon the media for anything. The media has become corrupt and they are working for prince of the power of the air. We forget that the devil has control over the second heavens. Why do you think that all of the major news outlets say the same thing? TV, Newspaper, and internet... They are speaking with one unified voice, whatever the devil wants out there, he speaks to them and they put it out there. Look at what the press has done during this election cycle. How long have we been trying to get family values talked about and respected by the American Press? For a long time, but as soon as they find some dirt on a Conservative Christian that's when they choose to all collectively bring this information out. But find some dirt on someone they like, and they will cover that thing up like you wouldn't believe.

Look at the difference in how they reported on Sarah Palin and how they reported on Barak Obama. Scandalous! But the Church is not wise enough to see that all of these media outlets and the prince of the power of the air are tied together. Just like the principality of gog, magog and the antichrist spirit are tied together. For fear of being called a racist the American Press refused to say anything negative against the 'black liberal' politician. They did not do the job that the press is supposed to do by properly bringing to light all of the information about Barak Obama. While many on the Republican and Conservative sides have cried foul and conspiracy, I see the agenda of God at work. Anyone who has studied politics can see some of the obvious faults of Barak Obama, but it is rather curious to me how the American Press down played all of these factors and character traits.

The error doesn't stop there; there are some in the Church who believe that we are supposed to remain neutral when it comes to elections. They refuse to affiliate with a party, they refuse to give their opinion and they want other people to do the same. This puts the Church in a rather difficult place because if you look at Biblical examples, the Church was absolutely a part of politics. God was all the time sending prophets to kings and leaders in the government telling them different things. There were Godly and ungodly political leaders alike and God didn't have a problem sending them a word. Sometimes they were good words and more times they were words of correction and discipline. It boggles the mind to know that so much can be tainted, twisted and corrupted but God knows all and sees all.

This error is the same error that was committed by the Church in Jesus day. They were looking for a king to come in and rid them of the high Roman taxes and the oppression that they were going through as Jewish citizens in Roman occupied territory. The problem with this is that Jesus came back as the Lamb because He had to die on the Cross. When the people didn't get what they wanted out of Jesus they had Him crucified. It really wasn't Pilate that had Jesus put to death it was the people. When you study this out and look at what's really going on it is a sign that Jesus is going to return but this time He is not coming back as a Lamb. He is coming back as a Lion and He is going to tear some things up because it was built on demonic foundations.

I like to tell people all the time when they are bound in this doctrine, "God doesn't need you to do anything." He doesn't need you to take up arms, He doesn't need you to storm the White House, He doesn't need you to go in and perform a violent takeover of this government. He has His angelic army and He has His Holy Spirit. To walk around in the arrogance that God needs a man to do anything is laughable. People who are caught up in this teaching are really bound and if you examine their life style closely they are not in the Spirit, they are really worldly, and they don't ever pick up their Bible.

There is another teaching that is pretty deep into the Church and that is the teaching that God only loves. He doesn't do anything bad, doesn't allow anything bad to happen to anyone and everything is just flowers and rainbows all the time. So, the problem with this is that if there is any kind of conflict that arises where someone is not doing what they need to do, you can't ever correct that behavior because a loving god would never be harsh or critical or judgmental. And they believe this so deeply that when reality hits them in the face they don't know how to handle this. They don't expect for God to correct them. They don't expect for God to be angry with them and when He does they quit God and leave Him.

This really affects them because when God tries to approach them and tell them what He is doing in the earth they don't want to receive it. God would never allow children to starve in Africa, God would never allow this country to be taken over by evil, and God would never allow 9-11 to happen because He loves us. This is sad also because it keeps people in bondage to this teaching that cannot be found in Scripture. All of these teachings have their roots in the demonic realm. The enemy knew what our weaknesses are and he exploits our misconception of who God is to his advantage. Now this teaching is used as the basis for the next totally demonic teaching that is out there and that is the "Don't judge me" teaching.

Don't judge me because only God can do that but because He is so loving and kind God won't do that. God is love I am good and can continue on in my sin. The don't judge me person in many ways believes that there is no judgment whatsoever. They believe that God is so merciful that He will just wave His hands and grant excuses to everyone who is caught in a lifestyle that is not Godly. So, the train of thought is that you get a pass and continue to do your thing without punishment but God does not work that way. He does judge you and does place good leaders in your life to bring discipline and correction into your life so that you can follow Him down the right path.

All of these different teachings and thought patterns are what is corporately wrong with the Church in the United States. It is these teachings in part and in whole that give birth to an atmosphere of permissiveness and sin. This occurs because no one in leadership will address a person who is in sin because of the fear of offending them. This has tied the hands of God so to speak because He has been promising to send a strong anointing into His houses. God will not dwell in His fullness in the presence of sin. Sin when it is unconfessed and unrepented of will cause the real deep glory of God to leave. The sad fact is that all across this nation the Glory of God has left. What's even sadder is that many in the Church do not understand that God's glory left. They are still operating in their programs and their agendas.

I believe that because the Church has so many openings in its teachings and there is an unwillingness of leadership to get Holy. Since these openings cannot be addressed the enemy has embedded himself into many of the Churches leaders. This has caused so much confusion, so much division that many faithful people have walked out the front door of the door church and have not been back. This problem goes much deeper because when your teachings are not sound, it can open the door for greater deceptions to take place and thereby leaving the Church to be subject to many voices speaking in place of the Spirit of God.

Dr. Rebecca Brown in her book, *"He Came to Set the Captives Free"* stated that it was nothing for satanist's and witches to go into the houses of God. They would become leaders and teachers and spread confusion and increase teachings that are incorrect doctrinally. Now enter the modern day prophetic movement. Many in the Body of Christ are learning to hear God's voice and this is good but there are some fake prophetic voices that are out there leading many people astray. They are even responsible for saying and doing things that are contrary to the Bible. The excuse being given is that they heard god say to them that it was Ok to do. Anytime you hear a voice and it tells you to do something contrary to the Bible that voice should not be followed. However there are those in the Body of Christ who don't know God and they are innocently subject to this foolishness.

There are those in the Church who are sent straight from the enemy and they are using their ministries to sow and bring confusion into the Church. They have a direct tie with the enemy of the Cross and because of this he can cause God's people to be deceived. This should not be able to occur but many in the Church do not study to show themselves approved. They allow for someone else to spoon feed them the Word and even worse they are still on the milk of the Word. Often the enemy can come in with slick words and nice sounding messages to tickle the ears of God's people and bring them into a place of total confusion.

If you look at what has gone on with the homosexual agenda it becomes plain. They have taken peoples misconception about God's love and changed God's law so that it causes people to say that homosexuality is an acceptable practice in God's eyes. They have convinced people with key words and phrases by saying that God approves of love, God approves being in a covenant relationship, God wants fidelity, so what wrong with homosexuality? The argument is smooth and it's designed to pull your attention away from what thou shalt not do.

In the case with the election of 2016 many in the Church rightly looked at the history and the character of each of the candidates and both were bad. Both of the top candidate's histories are filled with things that are less than Godly. This has caused much division in the Church because there is not a clear vision as to what we are to ask for in God. We are taking our past elections and our past experiences and overlooking things that should be obvious and making our decisions based upon this. It should be simple. It should be the choice between light over darkness but we don't know or understand the mind and heart of God. We should.

What the Church does not want to recognize is that there is a history of sin in the leadership of the Church that has been unrepented. There is a refusal to enact and follow a standard of holiness because there is no fear of God. The fear of God has left because the presence of God has left and there are times when the sermons delivered from the pulpits of this nation have no anointing in them or behind them because the one carrying the message is not anointed to carry it. You have to have to walk in spiritual integrity so that you can carry the anointing as you minister it to the people.

Mark 16:15-18 {NKJV}
15 And He said to them, "Go into all the world and preach the gospel to every creature. 16 He

> who believes and is baptized will be saved; but he who does not believe will be condemned. [17] And these signs will follow those who believe: In My name they will cast out demons; they will speak with new tongues; [18] they will take up serpents; and if they drink anything deadly, it will by no means hurt them; they will lay hands on the sick, and they will recover."

There has to be a belief by the one preaching the Word for it to have the power to activate the anointing in the Word. This is characteristic of the leadership in the Church as well because there are many who are just giving the sermon as a part of their job. They don't have a relationship with God themselves. This is their vocational profession. They only care or are concerned with delivering a good sermon and the applause and accolades of the people. Pleasing God is not in their thought process. The reason being is that they need to keep "butts in seats." We have to confess the reality of this truth and that is that some, not all, but some mega-churches are really experiments in socialization. They don't have the Spirit of God, they only have programs and the leadership in such places is geared towards making sure that people keep coming back.

This is radically different from a John the Baptist who didn't care what the people thought he only spoke what was on his heart to say from the Father. He lost his life because he told Herod that he was sleeping with his sister and it was a sin. We need this mentality to come back into the leadership in the Church such that they only care about pleasing God and not tickling the ears of the people. I am sure that John the Baptist would be thrown out of most Churches today. They would not endure the harshness of his tone, the violence with which he demonstrated the power of God, nor the gruffness of his personality. It would offend them to their core.

You have to know that not everyone in Church leadership is there from God. They could be a plant from the enemy to bring corruption into the Body. Because we are so forgiving and so willing to accept anyone it takes a long time for the Body of Christ to actually weed out anyone who is not of God. This is sad because so many people have been destroyed because the gift of discernment was not allowed to move in the midst of God's people. If we had the gift of discerning of spirits flowing and active like it should be in the Church then a lot of these deceptions would not have a leg to stand on. This has cost the Church so much in the way of time, respect, honor, and integrity.

There is an agenda amongst some of the leaders of the Church in regard to this election and it really centers on financial prosperity. Some of the leadership in the Church is motivated by money. Some of the leadership prophesied that Donald would win just because he was a millionaire and they believed that that would open the door to everyone else becoming a millionaire. They have in turn become blinded by his hard work and success. They got it right but got it wrong at the same time. Some in the Church missed the voice of God; they missed the true prophets of God because of chasing after money. A lot of leaders are hurting financially their Churches are hurting and they see that there people are hurting. So out of this hurt, wrong motive and agenda some in the Church prophesied that Donald would win.

This is where the Church needs to become honest. This is where those who are true need to admit that what they said was right but it was done out of a wrong heart. There are things that God has set in motion that He is going to do through Donald and they will be good things for the Church. But we must be aware that there are things that God is going to use Donald to do that will bring about corrections to the Church. Just because we have a God fearing man in the White House does not mean that the Church gets a pass and can continue business as usual. The Church must seek God and fall upon the "Rock" before the "Rock" falls upon it, the "Rock" being Jesus Christ.

> **Matthew 21:44 {NKJV}**
> [44] And whoever falls on this stone will be broken; but on whomever it falls, it will grind him to powder."

You can't fix what God wants broken until you fix what God wants fixed. Sounds like a mouth full. Yes, it is. We have the cart before the horse. We as a believers feel that money solves all problems and because we see people with money doing and enjoying life we naturally assume that they have no problems. We shouldn't do this but we do. I feel like one of the major mistakes of the leadership in the Church today is that they ignore what some would say are "negative" prophetic words. If anyone hears anything "negative" it is immediately thrown out and the person who gave the "negative" prophecy is taken in for counseling and then brainwashing. This is sad because if we don't know who our God is and what He can do we will miss Him.

You can't fix the problems of the world with money. They can only be fixed with God. Church leaders of today have slipped into this mindset and it is worldly. I have to inform you that we missed our opportunity to be blessed under good circumstances. The opportunity came through George W. Bush. Now, I believe that God is going to cause us to be blessed but under adverse circumstances. When we look at Joseph, he was sold into slavery by his brother's jealousy. They were jealous of their father's love for Joseph. I believe that God has many Joseph's who are waiting in the wings to be used by Him to manifest the goodness of God. They are pure in heart. They have no hidden agenda.

The Church has to get rid of its agendas and pick up God's agenda. The people were given their choice in the 2008 election. God spoke prophetically to my Pastor and said, **"The people want a king and I am going to give them a king and watch what the king does to them."** This was sad because this is an example of how the Body of Christ had their own agenda.

This was a warning that the Church did not see nor hear because they were too caught up in the flesh desiring what they thought was good and in turn our nation has fallen behind a painted picture that is now being revealed for what it is, total deception. Unfortunately, what God has been saying to us for a long time is that He wants us to straighten up. He wants us to be submitted to His will and plan.

There is a penalty for sin. When those in leadership realize this, and get serious about leading the people, they will be connected to the heart of God. God is doing a lot of exposing of sin. He has been working with the Church for quite some time now to bring all of the darkness into the light. If you would see and study what God has done in the Bible, you would see that every sin had a price. You cannot ignore the patterns that God has set in the Bible. Every one of them will be fulfilled. We are in a time of major prophetic fulfillment. The Bible is being fulfilled and the Church in this nation is a part of that. I believe that God is using us to cause Israel to turn back to Him. I believe that the gifts and the power of God are going to start increasing as the Church here in this nation goes through this time of judgment that we are headed into.

We are entering into a time of trouble and turmoil like we have never seen before. We are being judged. This is the elephant in the room that leaders in the Church want to ignore. This is the thing that God wants us to fix. We have to stop ignoring the truth that God is judging us. This keeps us from hearing the heart and voice of God. These judgments that are coming are meant to get us back on track but also meant to show us who our God really is. He is God. He is Righteous. He is Holy. We have to give Him what He wants. He wants all of us.

Corporately, the enemy knows that we are being judged. He understands this and he is using this against us. Because we refuse to walk in the truth and take our lickings that are coming to us; we are prolonging the day of wrath that is stored up for us.

> **2 Samuel 24:10-17 {NKJV}**
> [10] And David's heart condemned him after he had numbered the people. So David said to the LORD, "I have sinned greatly in what I

have done; but now, I pray, O LORD, take away the iniquity of Your servant, for I have done very foolishly."

¹¹ Now when David arose in the morning, the word of the LORD came to the prophet Gad, David's seer, saying, ¹² "Go and tell David, 'Thus says the LORD: "I offer you three *things;* choose one of them for yourself, that I may do *it* to you."'" ¹³ So Gad came to David and told him; and he said to him, "Shall seven years of famine come to you in your land? Or shall you flee three months before your enemies, while they pursue you? Or shall there be three days' plague in your land? Now consider and see what answer I should take back to Him who sent me."

¹⁴ And David said to Gad, "I am in great distress. Please let us fall into the hand of the LORD, for His mercies *are* great; but do not let me fall into the hand of man."

¹⁵ So the LORD sent a plague upon Israel from the morning till the appointed time. From Dan to Beersheba seventy thousand men of the people died. ¹⁶ And when the angel stretched out His hand over Jerusalem to destroy it, the LORD relented from the destruction, and said to the angel who was destroying the people, "It is enough; now restrain your hand." And the angel of the LORD was by the threshing floor of Araunah the Jebusite.

¹⁷ Then David spoke to the LORD when he saw the angel who was striking the people, and said, "Surely I have sinned, and I have done

> wickedly; but these sheep, what have they done? Let Your hand, I pray, be against me and against my father's house."

When you look at David, he knew that he sinned. He was in agreement that judgment needed to be sent to correct the situation. The only way for God's wrath to be appeased was for him to be punished. God sent that wrath and a multitude of people died but the judgment satisfied God's anger.

If the leadership in the Church would recognize this truth, we possibly could be spared the harsh judgments that are coming our way. But because of foolery and private agendas many innocents in the Body of Christ are going to suffer more. They are already suffering because they are in bondage but now they will be suffering because of the judgment that is coming. This did not have to be. The 2016 Election brought exposition to what is really wrong with the Church and God is about to move to correct this.

5

POLITICAL PARTIES

Smoke & Mirrors: You Must Always Look at the Other Hand!

In George Washington's Farewell Address, he warned his fellow Americans about the dangers of political parties. He said, "The alternate domination of one faction over another, sharpened by the spirit of revenge, natural to party dissension, which in different ages and countries has perpetrated the most horrid enormities, is itself a frightful despotism." He claimed the partisanship would lead to inter-political conflict, divide the nation, and give rise to cases of tyranny.[12]

----

[12] http://www.constitutionfacts.com/founders-library/first-party-system/

This is a powerful statement by the first President of this nation. They very thing that George warned us would happen has happened. The parties are constantly fighting with each other over power. The desire to lead this nation righteously does not exist in the party elites. Our nation's founding fathers would protest the way this nation has been divided by the parties. It does not matter which party has the power, the goal is the same by both, domination. When the Democrats have power, they dominate the Republicans and vice versa.

This domination in effect has created a monarchy. The founding fathers did not want a monarchy. This is why they left England. They wanted freedom from tyranny. They did not want a system that would create and set up kings. They developed a way for all men to live peaceably together without the domination that comes from a king. We may not call any one-person king in this nation but the behaviors of the parties have created a virtual monarchy. This virtual monarchy has enslaved this nation because of the disintegration of integrity of our leaders.

One of the most despicable things that has occurred in this nation is the disintegration of integrity. This disintegration of integrity is a cancer that is destroying the moral foundation on which this nation was created. The founding fathers placed checks and balances within our system that were meant to protect us from this degradation. The President has a check on Congress and the Courts. Congress has a check on the President and on the Courts. The Courts have a check on the President and Congress. The Party system was supposed to ensure fairness and the Free Press was supposed was to keep a check on them all. At the start of our nation every leader led an outward moral life. It was a duty to do so. This duty came with the responsibility of the office. Today morals are relative and are subject to changing with the seasons. We are living in times of great greed and corruption. Honor and integrity are just words that many politicians use to gain entry into office.

Once in office the politicians are swallowed up by the elites of their affiliated party. Without a strong moral foundation and support from the Lord. Many find themselves enslaved by their party. The agenda of the individual is easily co-opted and the will of the party takes preeminence over the will of the people. Party affiliation makes no difference in this scenario, the outcome is the same.

> **"Power tends to corrupt, and absolute power**
> **corrupts absolutely.**
> **Great men are almost always bad men."**
> *John Emerich Edward Dalberg Acton, first Baron Acton* (1834–
> 1902)

There is a great danger that comes from power. You have to be grounded morally and spiritually to not get corrupted by power. We all have the capacity to be evil. In certain circumstances this has been demonstrated by many politicians. To say "Great men are almost always bad men," speaks to the inability of most people to properly handle power. If one does not understand their limitations they can foolishly grab onto that "third rail" of their political party and literally be destroyed by the massive quantity of power that is available. I have been on the inside of the Delaware Republican party. I have worked in this machine and it is not nice. Money, power and corruption contribute to an endless cycle of impurity that caused me to see and experience first-hand this overwhelming pressure to succeed and rise up in the ranks of the party.

There are many who go into politics with the noblest of intentions. What most don't realize is that the money and power players in the parties seek to suck up and destroy the most innocent of souls. You have to prepare your heart to go into the depths of this world, if not you will lose your morals, your sanity and even your sense of right and wrong.

Some of you who are reading this book are good moral people and it is unfathomable to think that there are people out there who would slit your throat for power. So it is with those who get deeply connected in the world of politics. Money drives them. In their world money gives them power and power in the wrong hands becomes a very dangerous tool. There are wars fought for power and many a person has sold their soul to acquire power. Men and women who would have never thought of doing anything immoral when they get sucked into this trap often find it difficult to return to being human.

The political parties of this nation are many. I want to focus on the two leading parties, the Republican and the Democratic Parties. Both of these parties are founded on principals that are honorable. Anyone who wants to get into politics on the onset starts out because they want to help people. These parties do perform some good tasks for the citizens but that goodness slowly erodes away. These parties like to maintain absolute control over the candidates and their regions. If you want to be successful, you have to catch the eye of the kingmakers within the leadership of these parties. They are hidden but well organized and will do anything to maintain their power.

I learned this first hand as I started working my way through the ranks of the Republican Party in Delaware. I was always watched and scrutinized by those in leadership. I was not aware of this early on but I later learned that money was behind everything that was going on in Delaware and in this country. I remember watching and listening to everything and everyone. I heard conversations about different places, things, and people that were set up to move forward in the Party and to my surprise just as they stated things happened. I was naïve in a way because I really thought that the party was there to insure a fair process. They are not. I thought that I would get a fair shot and a chance to work my way through the ranks. This did not occur and after attendance at a party planning session I understood.

As nice as these leaders were to my face, they were even harsher and crueler behind my back. I had a contingent that was assigned to harass and ridicule every move I made. This contingent did the Parties dirty work. I quickly learned when people got out of line; they were assigned to put them back into line. At a planning party a leader came from the main headquarters in Washington. They were polite and even helpful but they openly discriminated against anyone who was not on their list of desirable candidates. They advised other candidates that everyone is welcome in the Republican but they just need to make sure that those who were less physically attractive were placed in the back or allowed to feel like they were apart. The term that was used was "Uncle Festers" Keep the Uncle Festers in the back so that they don't cost you or the party the election. We will ignore their character and just use them to do labor for the party. The Party doesn't care about people it only cares about keeping its power.

We watched this same ugly thing all the way through this election cycle this year. It was very clear that no matter what Donald said or did the Republican Party would never like him and never support him. They actively fought against him and did everything they could to slander him and run him down. It was sad to see but I believe they were responsible for everything negative that was leaked into the press while he was campaigning against the other candidates during the primaries. Instead of listening to what Donald was saying and getting behind him they chose to split the party because he didn't fit what they thought a president should look like. In the parties mind Donald was not presidential enough. Their thought process was simple and obvious; if Donald wins we will not be able to control him. So we must stop him and hinder him so that he does not win. They knew Donald would change their system and remove the big Party leaders. By the grace of God Donald endured the all that they administered against him and now he is on top of the food chain.

Rush Limbaugh opined the following:

In 2014, Republicans said, "Look, Obama still has the White House. Yeah, you gave us the House, but he's still got the White House. We can't stop him. We need the Senate." In 2014, landslide Republican turnout, landslide Republican win. Between 2010 and 2014, the Democrats lost over 1,000 seats in the House, in the Senate, state legislatures, governorships, was it massive. Still the Republicans who were elected on the promise that they were gonna fight, fight back, try to stop, didn't.

And that's all she wrote. Republicans had done everything that had been asked. The Republican voters had been asked, we need the House, fine, we gave it to 'em. We need the Senate. Fine. And even after they got the Senate, "Well, you know, Obama's still in the White House. There's really nothing we can do. 'Cause we don't have a veto-proof majority." So, no matter what we did, no matter how many things they asked us to do and we did, they fell back on the "it's still not enough" and there wasn't any serious opposition to the leftist Obama agenda." [13]

The revelation that Rush has was quite stunning. We have to change the way that we look at the parties. I am picking on the Republican Party at this point but both Parties are the same way. The Democratic Party needs to change as well. The Democratic Party is pushing the pro homo-sexual and transgender agenda. They are doing this despite overwhelming evidence that this this is a small segment of this nation.

The balance of power has shifted over the last eight plus years from a democratically run to a Republican run political system. Here is the truth. Both parties wind up

---

[13]http://www.rushlimbaugh.com/daily/2016/10/17/any_other_republican_would_ve_folded_by_now_but_trump_keeps_fighting_back

doing the same thing. Both parties wind up stealing money from the people, not doing what they promised, and then blame-shifting to say, "If we only had more of this and if we only had more of that we could really help the people." Rush calls these people out and tells it like it is. The people of this nation showed with this 2016 election that they are tired of being lied and ignored by the parties. Rush illustrates this beautifully and you must see in this case that not only did the Democrat elites do this but the Republicans elites did this as well. They did not want to lose their power. It was more important for them to keep power than to lose it.

I observed this type of behavior on the local level as well; the Party leaders for the Republicans in Delaware would make deals that just didn't make sense. Beau Biden was the Democratic Attorney General and common sense would say that as a Republican you run someone against him to try and take his seat. The party leaders said no, they had a made a side deal with the Democrats if they would let Biden run unopposed they would give the Republicans a token of appreciation. This occurred in race after race throughout that year.

This sounds contrary to the American dream and it is. This doesn't seem like a healthy spirit of competition was allowed to run its courses and determine the victor. The races have been fixed and corrupted by the parties. You must always watch what the other hand is doing. There were so many side deals taking place that there wasn't any room for good honest people to come in and participate. I felt bad as I watched this go on time after time with race after race. There are good people who are trying to do the right thing and the Party because these people didn't look like them, think like them, and act like them had shut down their races and effectively their chances for making a difference in the community. Our founding fathers believed in the market place of ideas. They believed that everyone should have a fair chance to enter the system.

Some would say that this is how it is supposed to be but is it really? Is one group of people supposed to be lords and monarchs over another group of people? No, they are not. We have to have a system that is open and fair. The Tea Party started a fire under the Republicans because the good honest people were tired of waiting on the dirty leadership within the Republican Party to make the right decision and help people win. The Tea Party started seeing that something wasn't right with the system. I believe that God was trying to work within the system but the power was just too much for the ones on in the inside. They craved that power, they needed that power and as much as this sounds like a conspiracy theory, I am telling you that it is the truth.

I have seen races where a Tea Party Republican was harassed and threatened to get out of a race because the leadership in the Republican Party did not want them to win the spot. How this breaks down is this person running for the office was a Republican and a part of the Tea Party. The main leaders in the Republican Party saw these people as a threat and felt like they were trying to steal their power from the Republicans so they shut their races down. They threw mud, they had people accuse them of wrong doing and they set up people who had no chance of winning run against these good people. What this really boils down to is the Republican Party had more money so they could literally outspend the honest person and causes them to lose the race that they were in.

Do you ever feel like somethings wrong but can't prove it? You can feel it in the atmosphere; you can feel it all around you but just can't figure it out. I believe that's God trying to get you to see that there is something else going on in the atmosphere around about you. When you at look both parties there is a culture within these parties that is elitist in nature. They are exclusive. If you don't belong to them, you will not be helped along in anything that you do. They smile, they look you in your face, have the appearance of helping you but all along they literally want nothing to do with you. Many times, both Parties appear before the people as wanting to do what is right but often they have a secret agenda that they are working to fulfill. If you are not part of the clique then you don't get the secret memos and invites to the secret meetings that go on.

I find it fascinating that as you surf through all forms of media, everyone says the same things. Radio talk show hosts pointed this out many years ago and if you are not paying attention you yourself can become a part of this system. I was dismayed at first to understand that the Democratic Party released a set of talking points to their people and everyone followed those points. There was never any independent thought. If a candidate expressed an idea that was independent from the talking points they were chastised or criticized until they got back in line with the rest. They are in perfect unity and are very well organized because they want to keep their power.

Does this mean that the person who is not liked by the Party cannot win? Absolutely Not! It does mean that they must work harder at winning than the person who has the backing of the Party. There are several candidates that won offices in 2012 that I know specifically the party leaders actively fought against. These people were affiliated with the party but weren't a part of the in crowd in the party. To the parties utter dissatisfaction some of these people won their campaigns. One race in particular stands out to me. He is a good man, an honest man who works for the people. He is a council man that has a lot of smarts. The Party often made fun of him and did not support him at all and it was because of his looks. He didn't fit their mold. He was an "Uncle Fester" that they tried to keep in the background. He knew this but still pushed on. He knew this but did not let them get to him. He won his race. Ronald Reagan did the very same thing. He didn't bow down to what the party said. He had character and did what was right in his heart.

I don't have first-hand knowledge of events like this in the Democratic Party but what I have seen in this race for President causes me to believe that the same struggle goes on in that side as well. On a national level, I watched Bernie compete and campaign against Hillary. He seemed like a viable candidate even though he was of Jewish origin and an admitted socialist, I was really hoping that he would get the nomination and take Hillary's spot. This did not occur because the Party made a deal with Hillary in the 2008 election. I believe that they asked her to step aside and let Obama win the races in 2008 and 2012 and after this they would put her up in 2016 to come in and take over. She allowed this to happen. There were so many stories put out there that she did not have money and she really did not want to run for office. I didn't believe any of them. Bernie was asked to come to the White House and it was all over after that he backed out of the race.

> **While several of Sanders' Democratic colleagues in the Senate think it's time Sanders gave up his quest, Vice President Biden said people should "give him time" to make that decision.**
>
> **House Minority Leader Nancy Pelosi was also conciliatory on Thursday, telling reporters that Sanders "has to make his own decisions."**
>
> **"He knows what's on the line," Pelosi said. "And he should be treated no differently than other candidates. He should be allowed the opportunity and the respect on how he brings us to a place that helps us advance the causes he's been fighting for."**
>
> **Sanders will also meet later Thursday with Senate Democratic leader Harry Reid, and holds a rally in Washington on Thursday evening, in advance of the Washington, D.C., Democratic primary next Tuesday.[14]**

All of these people had the appearance of supporting Bernie but they were sending messages to him to get out of Hillary's way. I think that they made him an offer that he could not refuse. I think where the climate is at politically a person of Jewish descent would not be welcome in the

---

[14] http://www.npr.org/2016/06/09/481387404/bernie-sanders-goes-to-the-white-house

White House. I believe that things have been set in place by our leaders to cause hatred and violence to start occurring against our Jewish brothers and sisters.

What's now coming to light is Bernie's wife alleged illegal land deal.

> **But the facts in the case do not fit well with Mr. Sanders's populist image. The charges revolve around a $6.5 million bank loan, that was obtained with a promise that <u>college donors would quickly pay back</u> at least $2.6 million of the debt. They did not, Ms. Sanders was ousted, and the college went belly up. The senator had already taken some grief last year for purchasing a $575,000 vacation home on Lake Champlain, to complement his house in Burlington and his rowhouse on Capitol Hill.**[15]

It's crazy because the Democrats get the credibility for being the first party to support minorities and people of color but that is completely wrong. It's crazy because the Democrats get the credibility for being the first party to support minorities and people of color but that is completely wrong. Everywhere down through history the Democratic Party has done everything in its power to oppress minorities and people of color. This is sad because

---

[15] https://www.nytimes.com/2017/07/15/us/politics/bernie-sanders-jane-sanders-investigation-burlington-college.html?mcubz=0

they really make you feel like they care. They make you feel like you have a voice and are a part. I have learned that while you are listening to them you must constantly watch their mouths and know up front that you are being lied to. But don't stop there you also need to watch what the other hand is doing. Because they are saying the right thing because they focus- grouped it and found out what people want to hear. They then take this knowledge and while they are stroking these people's egos with one hand the other hand is committing evil and advancing an agenda that is destructive to this country.

When you looked at the Republican Party and the Democratic Party it was clear that decisions had been made prior to Donald and Hillary running for office on which they would support. What's interesting to note was that it was clear from the outset that the Democratic Party elites were fully behind Hillary. The Republican Party did not want Donald to be there candidate and they actively fought against him every step of the way. Within the party was a group called "Never Trumpers." They were never going to be convinced that Donald would be the candidate for them. The Republican Party thought they were going to give us another Bush. They were wrong. Donald was not going to allow this to happen. Donald had the stamina and the push to fight against the party and this is what they did not like about him. He is not just gonna lie down and quit. He was in this to win the race.

Rush Limbaugh says this so eloquently:

Believe me, folks, this fight is exclusively about that the Republican Party has let down its primary supporters. By primary, I mean base. It has let them down. It has promised and not delivered. And the establishment, they're part of it and they circle the wagons here and they focus fire on Trump as a degenerate, as a reprobate, and they fire all of these usual political weapons.

They use every trick in their book. Okay, he hates women. War on Women. He's a racist. He's a sexist. He's a bigot. The Republican base has heard this said about every nominee that we've nominated, and they know it is total BS every time it's thrown around. Mitt Romney was not a sexist, a racist, he didn't hate women, he didn't hate animals, he didn't kill women, didn't do anything of the sort. Republicans didn't fight back, Republican base livid.

Ditto, George Bush. George Bush lied, people died, George Bush is Hitler, they could do books on assassinating George Bush. Republican voters know it's not true, George Bush a fine man, may have been wrong on immigration, but he was not the reprobate that the Democrats make him out to be, but there was no push-back, no fighting back. Republican voters disappointed and let down again. And so it goes.

So everything they're throwing at Trump, every Republican voter has heard it said about every Republican nominee since they've been alive. There's not one thing new. They got rid of speakers of the House. They got rid of others by claiming women -- Meanwhile, they on the Democrat side embrace and harbor their abusers and rapists. They lie about others. The female candidate for president on the Democrat side has attacked and bullied and threatened women who came forward, and the Republicans don't say so. Donald Trump does. [16]

Until we as citizens stand up and fight against the Parties we will continue to experience their control over us. It is not right that a few people dictate to the many what is supposed to happen. It is not right that those in this country are subjected to the wants of the few. This nation was supposed to be a representative government, where everyone's voice is heard. The Party system is not corrupt in and of itself but those people how have gained power are using it to their advantage.

If the Democratic and Republican Parties would have listened to its base supporters our country would not be in the mess that it is in today. It's fair to say that the blame should be shared on both sides of the aisle. We are all responsible for the things that go on within this nation. There are things we should be up in arms about but we have been lazy in trusting that those in power and leadership are operating under honor and integrity. When there is no honor or integrity our system will fail and it will not accomplish what our founding fathers wanted it to accomplish.

---

[16]http://www.rushlimbaugh.com/daily/2016/10/17/any_other_republican_would_ve_folded_by_now_but_trump_keeps_fighting_back

I don't place my hope in our government or its leaders. One of the fundamental questions that believers have been asking is how do we follow someone who is corrupt? This is a valid question and there is no easy answer to this. If you go based upon scripture you would have to consider the following:

> **Romans 13:1-7 {NKJV}**
> 13 Let every soul be subject to the governing authorities. For there is no authority except from God, and the authorities that exist are appointed by God. [2] Therefore whoever resists the authority resists the ordinance of God, and those who resist will bring judgment on themselves. [3] For rulers are not a terror to good works, but to evil. Do you want to be unafraid of the authority? Do what is good, and you will have praise from the same. [4] For he is God's minister to you for good. But if you do evil, be afraid; for he does not bear the sword in vain; for he is God's minister, an avenger to execute wrath on him who practices evil. [5] Therefore you must be subject, not only because of wrath but also for conscience' sake. [6] For because of this you also pay taxes, for they are God's ministers attending continually to this very thing. [7] Render therefore to all their due: taxes to whom taxes are due, customs to whom customs, fear to whom fear, honor to whom honor.

Based solely upon this passage of scripture, God puts the responsibility right back on us to follow those in authority. When you consider all that our government has done to destroy the innocents, this is a hard pill to swallow. No one likes this but the truth of the matter is that our elected officials are a reflection of who we are as a people. If we as individuals would not be tolerant of immorality and corruption in our individual lives, from our local elected officials, from our regional elected officials, to our national elected officials, from the party system elites and the presidential elected officials. This nation would be in a much better place. If we would stop being tolerant and throw these bums out of office that would send them a clear sign to straighten up but the Church remains silent on these issues.

We are to be like John the Baptist and have the strength and fire of Elijah but we don't want to hurt people's feelings. This is gonna be our downfall. We need to demand that these people in power live right and do right. The political parties see and know that no one is watching so they carry on with their destructive behaviors.

6

HILLARY R. CLINTON
Do Not Underestimate the Powers Behind Her!

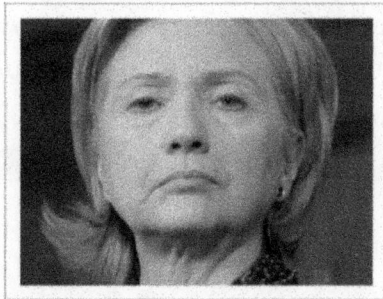

PROVERBS 30:18-20 (NKJV)
[18] There are three *things which* are too wonderful for me,
Yes, four *which* I do not understand:
[19] The way of an eagle in the air,
The way of a serpent on a rock,
The way of a ship in the midst of the sea,
And the way of a man with a virgin.
[20] This *is* the way of an adulterous woman:
She eats and wipes her mouth,
And says, "I have done no wickedness."

Jude 9 {NKJV}
9 Yet Michael the archangel, in contending with the devil, when he disputed about the body of Moses, dared not bring against him a reviling accusation, but said, "The Lord rebuke you!"

I fear the Almighty God with all of my heart. God has given His children wisdom, grace, and discernment. At times, we fail to walk in discernment. It is in those times that God's grace moves the most in our lives. Jude 9 should serve as a warning to all. You cannot in your own strength and your own power go against principalities and powers of darkness. If Michael the archangel refused to do this then you should apply the lesson that was communicated in Jude 9 to your life as well.

With this being said the principalities and powers in this woman pictured above are a force to be reckoned with. She is not innocent in anyway and she is one of the most evil women to ever walk the face of this earth. This may sound harsh and judgmental but the evidence speaks for itself. There are two biblical cases that I will cite as evidence that a person's sole purpose for being in this earth realm is for the purpose of doing some evil acts. Pharaoh and Judas are excellent proofs by which the case can be made that certain people are born on this earth to perform evil.

Romans 9:17 {NKJV}
17 For the Scripture says to the Pharaoh, "For this very purpose I have raised you up, that I

may show My power in you, and that My name may be declared in all the earth."

Exodus 9:12 {NKJV}
[12] But the LORD hardened the heart of Pharaoh; and he did not heed them, just as the LORD had spoken to Moses.

John 6:70-71 {NKJV}
[70] Jesus answered them, "Did I not choose you, the twelve, and one of you is a devil?" [71] He spoke of Judas Iscariot, *the son* of Simon, for it was he who would betray Him, being one of the twelve.

John 13:26-27 {NKJV}
[26] Jesus answered, "It is he to whom I shall give a piece of bread when I have dipped *it*." And having dipped the bread, He gave *it* to Judas Iscariot, *the son* of Simon. [27] Now after the piece of bread, Satan entered him. Then Jesus said to him, "What you do, do quickly."

It is clear from these scriptures that Pharaoh and Judas were born to be used by God to perform evil. Some in the Body of Christ find a way to "save" everyone. This is not scriptural because this is not the plan of God. There are many people who will not be redeemed. There are even angels who have fallen that will not be redeemed. The evidence is prevalent to suggest that Hillary is not redeemable.

Hillary is the wife of former President Bill Clinton. He served as president from 1992 to 2000. She was first lady and served this nation alongside her husband. They are a power couple in many ways. They both have accomplished a lot together.

When Hillary Clinton was elected to the U.S. Senate in 2001, she became the first American first lady to ever win a public office seat. She later became the 67th U.S. secretary of state in 2009, serving until 2013. In 2016, she became the first woman in U.S. history to become the presidential nominee of a major political party.[17]

Hillary was no slouch. She came up in a man's world and she learned to fight like a man. She learned how to take and give punches and keep on going.

Hillary was mentored by Saul Alinsky. Alinsky was one of the world's most radical individuals. Hillary's whole life has been dedicated to socialist/communist ends. The fact that the arguments and the anger fomented by Alinsky in the 40s, 50s and 60s are the same arguments and anger of today's Barack and Hillary model is telling. It speaks to how far they will go to get whatever power they desire.[18]

---

[17] https://www.biography.com/people/hillary-clinton-9251306
[18] See more at: https://www.conservativereview.com/commentary/2016/08/alinskys-daughter-here-is-the-truth-about-hillary-the-media-will-not-tell-you#sthash.rWYhoTCT.dpuf

During this election cycle former, republican presidential candidate Ben Carson exposed Hillary's background with Alinsky during the Republican debates.

> **His main concern, he told Chris Cuomo Wednesday morning on CNN's New Day, was that Clinton considered Alinsky her mentor, and had referred to his famous book Rules for Radicals in her college thesis. Alinsky, meanwhile, had once appeared to praise the devil. "On the dedication page, he acknowledged Lucifer in an admirable way, saying that he's the original radical who gained his own kingdom," Carson explained. "Please read the book, because it's very interesting how it uses controlled anarchy in order to change us from a democratic republic to a socialist society."[19]**

Here are quotes from Alinsky himself.

> **"Lest we forget at least an over the shoulder acknowledgment to the very first radical: from all our legends, mythology and history (and who is to know where mythology leaves off and history begins - or which is which), the very first radical known to man who**

---

[19]https://www.google.com/amp/www.vanityfair.com/news/2016/07/ben-carson-clinton-lucifer/amp

**rebelled against the establishment and
did it so effectively that he at least won
his own kingdom - Lucifer."**

**"To say that corrupt means corrupt the
ends is to believe in the immaculate
conception of ends and principles. The
real arena is corrupt and bloody. Life
is a corrupting process from the time a
child learns to play his mother off
against his father in the politics of
when to go to bed; he who fears
corruption fears life."** [20]

So, sitting under the mentorship of such a powerfully dark influence you can see how and why Hillary grew into the person she is today.

Hillary has been influenced by many dark people. She is a follower and fan of Margaret Sanger. Sanger was the founder of Planned Parenthood. Sanger opened the world's first birth control clinic in 1916 in New York City. She was a leading proponent of eugenics. [21] Eugenics is the study of or belief in the possibility of improving the qualities of the human species or a human population, especially by such means as discouraging reproduction by persons having genetic defects or presumed to have inheritable undesirable traits **(negative eugenics)** or

[20] https://www.goodreads.com/author/quotes/59314.Saul_D_Alinsky
[21] https://www.thegospelcoalition.org/article/9-things-you-should-know-about-planned-parenthood-founder-margaret-sanger

encouraging reproduction by persons presumed to have inheritable desirable traits **(positive eugenics)**.[22]

Sanger believed, "Morons, mental defectives, epileptics, illiterates, paupers, unemployables, criminals, prostitutes, and dope fiends ought to be surgically sterilized and if they choose live a life long existence in labor camps. In our modern times wouldn't something so barbaric be looked down upon? This is not a politically correct ideology. This is astounding. What's more astounding is that no one has challenged Hillary to disconnect from these ideologies. Hillary is praised as an activist for women and children.

Hillary has never disconnected herself with Sanger's beliefs. In fact, in 2009 Hillary was awarded the Margaret Sanger award by Planned Parenthood. The award was given for recognition of leadership, excellence and outstanding contributions to the reproductive health and rights movement. Hillary said, **"I admire Margaret Sanger enormously. Her courage, her tenacity, her vision... I am really in awe of her."**[23]

When you look at Hillary's life, it is virtual path of darkness and dissidence. Throughout her journey Hillary is always surrounded by scandal. It's interesting to note that while these scandals are all around her there are some consistent events that take place. Someone dies, someone goes to jail, and it's never Hillary. This is not just coincidence. This is because she is protected by

---

[22] http://www.dictionary.com/browse/eugenics
[23] https://www.thegospelcoalition.org/article/9-things-you-should-know-about-planned-parenthood-founder-margaret-sanger

principalities and powers that are using her to perform their dirty deeds. In each of these cases it mattered not how close you were to Hillary or how long you served her. If it was better for her that you be moved out of the way then you were moved out of the way, in whatever form that needed to take.

> **Vince Foster was deputy White House counsel and Hillary's friend and law partner who had connections to the Travelgate and Whitewater scandals. In 1993, Foster was found dead in a park with a fatal gunshot wound to his mouth. As World Net Daily (WND) reported, his suicide was the subject of much speculation and three official investigations.[24]**

Travelgate was the scandal that involved the White House travel office. The Clintons thought it necessary to falsely accuse seven employees of travel office so that they could hire and place their friends in those positions. These new employees took over the travel business of the White House. This also included removing the FBI from the office. This caused a huge stink. By the time all was said and done the original employees were re-instated in equivalent positions in the government. Hillary was the principal party responsible for these firings. The Whitewater scandal started as the real estate investments of Bill, Hillary and their associates. The scandal revealed that Bill Clinton pressured David Hale to loan Susan McDougal

---

[24] http://www.wnd.com/2015/05/here-they-are-hillarys-22-biggest-scandals-ever/

$300,000. This was fraud.   This scandal led to the death of Hillary's friend Vince Foster.

Hillary was named in a lawsuit brought by Peter Franklin Paul for allegedly directing to her 2000 Senate campaign an illegal, in-kind contribution from Paul that included a fundraiser at the exclusive Spago restaurant in Beverly Hills, a tea hosted at the Beverly Hills home of socialite Cynthia Gershman and a lavish, A-list, million-dollar-plus Hollywood gala honoring Bill Clinton. At the trial of Clinton's finance director for the 2000 senatorial campaign, David Rosen, the government told the jury Paul personally gave more than $1.2 million to produce the events.

Paul, a former business partner of Spider-Man creator Stan Lee who sued Bill for fraud and accused Hillary of hiding nearly $2 million in Senate campaign donations, alleged they sabotaged the media company he formed with Lee to get out of a $17 million agreement made with Bill Clinton to serve as an international promoter for the company after he left the White House. Paul was indicted in June 2001 for manipulating the price of the stock in his company, Stan Lee

Media, as it was collapsing. A judge determined Paul didn't profit from the attempt to save his company, but he accepted a plea bargain and served three years in prison.[25]

Everyone is familiar with the various sex scandals that took place featuring Bill as the perpetrator. While a hatred for Bill amongst some women ensued, a certain mystique and mystery surrounded Hillary. People began to wonder what was really going on in this relationship. Each and every time a mistress of Bill's would turn up; she would defend him and stand with him. It became clear that something was morally off about Bill & Hillary. World Net Daily reported the following:

The Clintons have been accused of hiring private investigators to not only dig up dirt on perceived adversaries – such as Juanita Broaddrick, the woman allegedly raped by Bill, and other abused women such as Gennifer Flowers, Kathleen Willey and Paula Jones – but to stalk, scare and threaten them. Willey asserts Hillary was behind a campaign of intimidation and harassment against her that fit a pattern employed against numerous other women whose claims of sexual impropriety or assault by Bill Clinton

---

[25] http://www.wnd.com/2015/05/here-they-are-hillarys-22-biggest-scandals-ever/

threatened   the   couple's   political
fortunes.[26]

There is so much that Hillary has had her hands in
and none of it is good.   Hillary as a person has been
reported as mean and ruthless with her staff and aides.   A
former Secret Service agent reveals the following:

> **"Hillary Clinton has a "Jekyll and
> Hyde" personality that left White
> House staffers scared stiff of her
> explosive — and even physical —
> outbursts, an ex-Secret Service officer
> claims in a scathing new tell-all.**
>
> **Gary Byrne, who was posted outside
> the Oval Office when Bill Clinton was
> president, portrays Hillary as too
> "erratic,   uncontrollable   and
> occasionally violent" to become leader
> of the free world..."[27]**

As we look into Hillary's world we continue to see
that it is filled with darkness. Not only from the people she
admires and respects but the people that she has around her.
My Pastor always says, "Spirit draws to spirit." What that
means is if you have a lustful spirit you will be drawn to
and comfortable with those who have a lustful spirit.   If
you have an angry spirit you will be drawn to and

---

[26] http://www.wnd.com/2015/05/here-they-are-hillarys-22-biggest-scandals-ever/
[27] http://pagesix.com/2016/06/05/tell-all-book-reveals-hillarys-erratic-uncontrollable-ways-in-the-white-house/

comfortable with other angry people. Hillary's circle is dark.

During this past election cycle, strong evidence came forward tying Hillary and her staff to witchcraft. Former Clinton insider Larry Nichols says:

> **"I know about once a month Hillary would go out to Los Angeles. And she did it so regular that it became a bit of an issue... 'Why's she always going?'"**

> **"Bill told me that she was going out there, she and a group of women, and she would be a part of a witch's church. Man, when Bill told me that, she could have hit me with a baseball bat. I tried to point out to him, 'Do you realize what would happen if that got out?' Of course, my job was to make sure it didn't get out."''**

> **"Now I don't know the day, if Hillary still partakes in the witch ritual, I don't know that I even know what the ritual was. But for the better part of many years, Hillary would go quite often, whether it was regularly once a month, or maybe once every couple of**

months, she would go out on the
weekend simply to be a part of it."[28]

Leon Podesta Hillary's campaign chairman was
exposed by a cyber phishing attack which revealed among
other things that Podesta was engaging in the practice of
spirit cooking.

> Spirit cooking is also an "occult
> practice used during sex cult rituals, as
> explained in the book "Spirit cooking
> with essential aphrodisiac
> recipes," *notes Mike Cernovich.*

> The revelation that John Podesta,
> Hillary Clinton's campaign chairman,
> is presumably interested in weird, gory
> occult ceremonies was too juicy for
> even WikiLeaks to ignore.

> "The Podesta's' "Spirit Cooking"
> dinner? It's not what you think. It's
> blood, sperm and breastmilk. But
> mostly blood," the organization
> tweeted.[29]

Hillary is also involved in other strange practices.

> Sources in the New York Police
> Department have indicated that the

---

[28] https://www.infowars.com/hillary-regularly-attended-witchs-church-clinton-insider-claims/
[29] http://www.exposingsatanism.org/hillary-clintons-witchcraft/hillary-clintons-witchcraft-part-8/

FBI has discovered evidence on the laptop shared by Huma Abedin and estranged husband Antony Weiner that suggest former President Bill Clinton wasn't the only Clinton who frequented convicted pedophile Jeffrey Epstein's Caribbean island, known as "Orgy Island."

Democrat presidential nominee Hillary Clinton allegedly visited the island, too.

Blackwater USA founder and retired Navy SEAL Erik Prince claimed a "well-placed source" in the New York Police Department told him that among the 650,000 emails discovered on Weiner's laptop was evidence that Hillary Clinton traveled to the island several times, Breitbart News reported.[30]

Hillary's husband Bill is seen on video saying the following:

"And a special thanks to the members of the Roosevelt family who are here and the one who is not. Eleanor who made sure that the four freedoms were

---

[30] http://conservativetribune.com/hillary-orgy-island-bombshell/?utm_source=Facebook&utm_medium=TeaParty&utm_content=2016-11-05&utm_campaign=manualpost

included in the preamble to the universal declaration of human rights in 1948. I know that because as all of you famously learned when I served as President my wife now the Secretary of State was known to commune with Eleanor on a regular basis. And so she called me last night on her way home from Peru to remind me to say that that Eleanor had talked to her and reminded her that I should say that."[31]

Having seen the video myself, there was no smile, no hint of sarcasm on the part of Bill. There was extreme sincerity. No one in the audience laughed, snickered, or even hinted that what was being said by Bill was not serious. They all including Bill believed it.

Many have poo poo'ed the reality of Hillary being into witchcraft but there is all of this evidence and more. When Leon Podesta's emails were released by Wiki leaks you have to start honestly questioning what is going on with Hillary.

I believe that she is a part of the system that is tied to the antichrist. She is not the antichrist but she is working under the same spirit of antichrist that is prevalent in this world today.

> **1 John 2:18 {NKJV}**
> [18] Little children, it is the last hour; and as you have heard that the Antichrist is coming, even

[31] https://youtu.be/UMN72aXzdFg

> now many Antichrists have come, by which we know that it is the last hour.

The antichrist spirit is responsible for bringing about the destruction of nation of Israel and Christianity. The antichrist spirit is the spirit that all other spirits work under. It seeks to destroy the Kingdom of God wherever it is found. The antichrist spirit is the same spirit that was behind the extermination of the Jews during World War II. The antichrist spirit opens the door for lawlessness. There is no restraint to any desire.

There is a season coming where the antichrist spirit will be allowed to freely move within this nation. Prior to this election a framework and infrastructure were set up by Barack. This framework caused pro-islamic leaders to gain access to the deepest parts of our government. Hillary's deputy chief of staff Huma Abedin was one of those people.

> **Abedin has known ties to the Islamic Brotherhood. A group bent on destroying western civilization from within - and other Islamic supremacists. As World Net Daily (WND) has extensively reported, the Muslim Brotherhood and Islamic supremacist connections not only extend to Abedin's mother and father, who are both deeply tied to al-Qaida fronts, but to Abedin herself.**
>
> **As WND reported, a manifesto commissioned by the ruling Saudi Arabian monarchy places the work of**

an institute that employed Abedin at
the forefront of a grand plan to
mobilize U.S. Muslim minorities to
transform America into a Saudi-style
Islamic state, according to Arabic-
language researcher Walid Shoebat.

Abedin was an assistant editor for a
dozen years for the Journal of Muslim
Minority Affairs for the Institute for
Muslim Minority Affairs. The institute
– founded by her late father and
currently directed by her mother – is
backed by the Muslim World League,
an Islamic organization in the Saudi
holy city of Mecca that was founded by
Muslim Brotherhood leaders. The 2002
Saudi manifesto shows that "Muslim
Minority Affairs" – the mobilizing of
Muslim communities in the U.S. to
spread Islam instead of assimilating
into the population – is a key strategy
in an ongoing effort to establish
Islamic rule in America and a global
Shariah, or Islamic law, "in our
modern times.[32]

You cannot ignore the truth. There are powerful
principalities and powers working with Hillary. Hillary is
a part of a power cluster that is tied to many spirits but the
chief spirits associated with this power cluster are the

---

[32] http://www.wnd.com/2015/05/here-they-are-hillarys-22-biggest-scandals-ever/

ahab/jezebel spirit. The ahab/jezebel spirit under the antichrist spirit is the same combination that was in place when Jesus was alive. We are in for some serious challenges in the days ahead. The nature of Hillary and Bills relationship is demonic. Hillary being the jezebel and Bill being the ahab, without Bill there would be no Hillary and just like in the Bible without ahab there would be no jezebel.

> **1 Kings 21:25-26 {NKJV}**
> 25 But there was no one like Ahab who sold himself to do wickedness in the sight of the LORD, because Jezebel his wife stirred him up. 26 And he behaved very abominably in following idols, according to all *that* the Amorites had done, whom the LORD had cast out before the children of Israel.

Never before in the History of our country have we had such a clear demonic couple in power and leadership. The principality and power associated with the queen of heaven is tied directly to Hillary. They both fit the pattern of the jezebel/ahab story in the Bible.

> **Bob Larson says, "The spirit of Jezebel, a demonic force of sex, power, control, manipulation, and murder is one of the most prevalent spirits of our age. This powerful and cunning demon is male but masquerades as female in its most deceptive form. It is often aligned with its demonic companion Ahab, mimicking the ancient evil of the apostate king and queen of Israel depicted in I King, Chapters 18 – 21"**

They have been demonic from the very first time they began their careers in politics. Hillary and Bill have done more damage to the moral fabric of this country than anyone even begins to understand. Because of their open sin natures and practicing of witchcraft the gates of Hell have been opened up in the spirit realm and masses of demons have come in and infested this nation. The Word of God depicts her as a woman without conscience and unalterably opposed to the God of Israel, even in the face of spiritual defeat and judgment.

> **1 Kings 18:2-4 {NKJV}**
> ² So Elijah went to present himself to Ahab; and *there was* a severe famine in Samaria. ³ And Ahab had called Obadiah, who *was* in charge of *his* house. (Now Obadiah feared the LORD greatly. ⁴ For so it was, while Jezebel massacred the prophets of the LORD, that Obadiah had taken one hundred prophets and hidden them, fifty to a cave, and had fed them with bread and water.)

> **1 Kings 19:1-2 {NKJV}**
> 19 And Ahab told Jezebel all that Elijah had done, also how he had executed all the prophets with the sword. ² Then Jezebel sent a messenger to Elijah, saying, "So let the gods do *to me,* and more also, if I do not make your life as the life of one of them by tomorrow about this time."

> **1 Kings 21:11-16 {NKJV}**
> ¹¹ So the men of his city, the elders and nobles who were inhabitants of his city, did as Jezebel had sent to them, as it *was* written in the letters which she had sent to them. ¹² They

proclaimed a fast, and seated Naboth with high honor among the people. [13] And two men, scoundrels, came in and sat before him; and the scoundrels witnessed against him, against Naboth, in the presence of the people, saying, "Naboth has blasphemed God and the king!" Then they took him outside the city and stoned him with stones, so that he died. [14] Then they sent to Jezebel, saying, "Naboth has been stoned and is dead."

[15] And it came to pass, when Jezebel heard that Naboth had been stoned and was dead, that Jezebel said to Ahab, "Arise, take possession of the vineyard of Naboth the Jezreelite, which he refused to give you for money; for Naboth is not alive, but dead." [16] So it was, when Ahab heard that Naboth was dead, that Ahab got up and went down to take possession of the vineyard of Naboth the Jezreelite.

When you look at Hillary and Bill they appear together as one. They looked the part, played the part and managed the part of being married. Their marriage is something that many people have questioned. Many have wondered over the years why she stayed, why did she put up with his philandering ways? It is because ahab and jezebel are working together in unity to do the bidding of the antichrist spirit. The antichrist spirit is setting the stage not only in this nation but around the world so that the battle of all battles can take place.

The people in this nation refuse to see the truth for what it is because we live in a day when good is called evil and evil is called good. The massacre that is headed our way will be on a scale that we cannot comprehend. You need to be aware of what is really going on. You need to see that this has been in the works for a long time. This was all strategic and a set up by the devil himself.

Never in the history of this nation has one woman been so public and so blatant in her disregard for what is decent and moral. Hillary is enabled by some very strong principalities and powers that in the season ahead will wreak havoc upon this nation. Many have counted her out because she lost this election cycle and the one in 2008 to Barack. I would caution you not to do that. There has been a lot of work put into grooming and preparing this woman to take her place in the coming move of judgment against this nation. She will play an integral part in bringing this nation to its knees.

Never in the history of this nation has a woman advanced with so much power. This is not to be ignored. She must be watched. She must be prayed against with all fervency. Do not be skeptical but take every word that I am about to share with you into your heart and soul. There is something demonically special about this woman. She has a background in darkness and witchcraft that must not be ignored.

Hillary lost the 2016 Election. What went wrong? God intervened on our behalf. God stepped into this election and gave this nation one more opportunity to turn around and get ourselves right with God.

7

DONALD J. TRUMP
From Joker To Victor

What billionaire in their right mind would run for the office of the President of this nation? What billionaire would stop running his businesses to put up with constant rejection, harassment and ridicule all for the betterment of this nation? What billionaire would leave the comforts and luxuries that are equated with having wealth to save his nation? What man would successfully defeat a pool of seventeen Republican candidates and earn the nomination from the Republican Party to run against Hillary? What man would fight against a political machine that did everything they could to keep him from earning his place in the history books? What man would stand against a Free Press who was controlled by that machine? That man is Donald J. Trump.

Only God knows what drew Donald into the political arena. Many have speculated that it was for vanity. Others speculated that he needed personal validation. I don't believe any of these reasons are to bare. It doesn't make sense to any of his naysayers that Donald would seek the office of the President of this nation.   These people don't understand the blood that has been shed and the lives that have been given for this nation. This nation should always be prosperous. This nation should always have plenty. Donald knows this. Donald understands this. Donald like the many that voted for him knew that there were people in our government who were planted there to take this nation down. Donald chose to have the courage, the strength and the fortitude to not only fight against them but to stop them from destroying this nation.

Only time will tell if Donald will be successful or not. Donald has a lot of enemies and they all want him to disappear. This nation has been on a downward spiral for a long time.   The people of this nation are tired of being in this downward spiral. The people of this nation see what needs to be done and are astounded that our political leaders refuse to fix what is so obviously wrong.

> **"What truly matters is not which party controls our government, but whether our government is controlled by the people,"**

"January 20, 2017, will be remembered as the day the people became the rulers of this nation again.

"Americans want great schools for their children, safe neighborhoods for their families, and good jobs for themselves,"

"These are the just and reasonable demands of a righteous public. But for too many of our citizens, a different reality exists: Mothers and children trapped in poverty in our inner cities; rusted-out factories scattered like tombstones across the landscape of our nation; an education system flush with cash, but which leaves our young and beautiful students deprived of knowledge; and the crime and gangs and drugs that have stolen too many lives and robbed our country of so much unrealized potential. This American carnage stops right here and stops right now."[33]

These are the words of President Donald J. Trump after he was sworn in. Donald understands what the people have been asking for. A return to what's right, a return to

---

[33] https://www.biography.com/people/donald-trump-9511238

the values that were held by our founding fathers and the generations that followed them. Donald believes, unlike Barack and Hillary, that the principles that this nation was built upon were not islamic principles, they were Godly principles. Donald made a decision to intervene and be a part of the solution. He is a man of action and those actions have caused Donald to be where he is at today.

There is corruption on all levels of this nation and until someone strong stops it that corruption will always be there. As discussed in previous chapters there are forces of darkness that have been seeking to destroy this nation from within. This election victory was a complete surprise to most. No one expected Donald to win.

> **"Nobody predicted this," said Chris Matthews on MSNBC.**
>
> **"I don't know one poll that suggested that Donald Trump was going to have this kind of night," said Jake Tapper on CNN.**
>
> **"He is still in this," said Chris Wallace of Fox News a few minutes after 9 p.m., adding, "and I'm not sure a lot of us thought he would be at this hour."**
>
> **Within a few hours, gentle humor had fallen away. "It is a white-knuckle kind of night," Norah O'Donnell said on CBS News. "You're either opening a second bottle of wine or you're brewing a new pot of coffee."**

A memorable moment occurred when Bill O'Reilly, the Fox News commentator who had been mostly absent from his channel's coverage on Tuesday, beamed into the set, tieless, through a camera set up in his Long Island home. At the time, Florida appeared to be trending toward Mrs. Clinton, but Mr. O'Reilly was not having it. "It's pretty much a dead heat," he said, jousting with Charles Krauthammer, a Fox News analyst who said he believed Mrs. Clinton still had the advantage.

CNN, by contrast, offered a tornado of a broadcast, with a constant whirl of breathless announcements, a nonstop musical score — drumbeats and synthesizer noises even accompanied the anchors' analysis — and a seemingly never-ending series of countdown clocks in the corner of the screen.[34]

I was up till 3 am on election night and I remember how stunned the media was. Perry Stone Jr. of Voice of Evangelism was given an interesting prophecy regarding this election. This was originally broadcast on the television program It's Supernatural by Sid Roth.

---

[34] https://mobile.nytimes.com/2016/11/09/business/media/media-coverage-election-day.html?referer=https://www.google.com/

"So, I start at looking at number 45, are y'all ready for this? This is crazy. If you take the 40 and the 5 in the Hebrew alphabet it's Ma. (pronounced Maaa) Not Mom but Ma. Do you know what the word Ma means? It means what? It means what?

Here's what gonna happen. Everybody mark this down. Whoever gets in? People are gonna say, "What?" "What?'' "How did this happen?" "What?" "What's going on?" watch it.

It was really hilarious... three days later all the major TV networks look at the screen and said, all the American people are saying what? And my wife just laughed at me and shook her head.

Biblical numbers have meanings. And they do correlate with the Hebrew alphabet which is God's alphabet. A lot of times in studying prophecy from the Hebraic perspective do we get hints, not necessarily a direct word but a hint to say look out for this. (Laughter) so look out for this. [35]

I love how this played out because no one saw this playing out the way that it did. He was the unlikely

[35] https://youtu.be/OIEmnBsXyZQ

candidate. To many he was a joker. Many people expected he would pull out of the race like Ross Perot. This made him the underdog and even though his message spoke for and to the people the party elites on both sides of the aisle never imagined a day where someone like Donald would be the President of this nation. However, God knew differently.

See what God used Kim Clement to say long before Donald arrived on the scene.

April 4, 2007 – Prophet Kim Clement

> **"This that shall take place shall be the most unusual thing, a transfiguration, a going into the marketplace, if you wish, into the news media. Where** Time **magazine will have no choice but to say what I want them to say.** Newsweek, **what I want to say.** "The View", **what I want to say.**
>
> **Trump shall become a trumpet, says the Lord. Trump shall become a trumpet. I will raise up the Trump to become a trumpet..."**

February 10, 2007 – Prophet Kim Clement

> **"There will be a praying president, not a religious one. For I will fool the people, says the Lord. I will fool the people, Yes, I will God says, the one that is chosen shall go in and they shall**

say "He has hot blood. For the Spirit of God says, yes, he may have hot blood, but he will bring the walls of protection on this country in a greater way and the economy of this country shall change rapidly, says the Lord of Hosts. Listen to the Word of the Lord. God says, I will put at your helm for two terms a President that will pray, but he will not be a praying President when he starts. I will put him in office and then I will baptize him with the Holy Spirit and My power, says the Lord of Hosts."[36]

Donald is a foolish thing who has been sent by God to confound the wise in the world and the wise in the Church.

> **1 Corinthians 1:27 (AMP)**
> 27 But God has selected [for His purpose] the foolish things of the world to shame the wise [revealing their ignorance], and God has selected [for His purpose] the weak things of the world to shame the things which are strong [revealing their frailty].

To say that God is using Donald to reveal ignorance is a beautiful thing. Donald has been selected by God for His purpose. Donald is not a stranger to politics. It had to be a part of his business dealings in the past and now that

---

[36] https://www.youtube.com/watch?v=OBo_BYKMSPE&app=desktop

he is President it will forever be a part of his life. Just because politics is involved that does not mean that the right things cannot be done. They can be done.

Our nation has gone to Hell in a hand basket over the past eight plus years because of the failed policies and agendas of the elites who are controlled by the principalities and powers associated with the antichrist spirit. These forces do not like Donald and are using every stratagem they can to make him appear that he does not know what he is doing. Donald is a foolish thing shaming the wise. The awesome thing about Donald is that he never was a politician. So, he has nothing to gain by playing politics. This made him an instant favorite amongst the people.

Donald is not so pure in heart but as you look throughout his life you can see that he has transitioned through his many epiphanies into the person that he is today. No one is perfect; the only one that was perfect was quickly put on a cross. The Bible says that our righteousness is as filthy rags. The reality is that God does not need Donald to be a Christian to speak through him or even use him. There are plenty of examples of this in the Bible. There are many Christians who have surrounded him and are supporting him but there are also many more Christians who are ridiculing him and putting him down. His lifestyle and character have proven to me that Donald will not deny Christ.

Donald is unique in so many ways. His greatest strength is that he is able to make his own decisions and he has a moral compass. It is clear from his time in office so far as President that he has a voice and he is not afraid to use it to speak up for what is right. The Church has lost its voice because it has things in common with the world. This commonness in the Church has shut up the voice of God and hampered the ability of God to speak through the Church. Fortunately for this nation Donald is cut from a different cloth.

Donald has the appearance of being rough around the edges. For those who don't understand him. All they see is someone who appears to be a prideful bully. Striking out at the weak and consuming everyone in his path. When you take an honest look at Donald you get an entirely different perspective. We already know that Donald is no stranger to work. If he were lazy the many failed businesses he has would be all that we know about him. However, this was not the final outcome of his life. Donald despite failed businesses and business ventures persevered the rough and tumble world of real estate.

"In 1971, he became involved in large, profitable building projects in Manhattan. In 1980, he opened the Grand Hyatt, which made him the city's best-known developer. In 2004, Trump began starring in the hit NBC reality series The Apprentice, **which also spawned the offshoot** The Celebrity Apprentice. **Trump turned his attention to politics, and in 2015 he announced his candidacy for president of the**

United States on the Republican ticket."[37]

Donald has the appearance of failing in his family life as well. Donald is currently married to Melania, but experienced the harsh reality of two failed marriages one from his first wife Ivana Trump and another from his second wife Marla Maples. Donald has found success in his third marriage with Melania. This success appears to be one of his epiphanies.

With his marriage to Melania secure Donald committed to developing his relationship with his family. Donald has three children with Ivana; Donald Jr, Ivanka, & Eric. Donald has his fourth child with Marla; Tiffany. Donald has his fifth child with Melania; Barron.

Everyone understands the dynamics that it takes these days to stay married, to raise a family and to still be a decent human being. To see Donald with his family today, you can see the fruit that has occurred in his life because he did not give up on searching and seeking to make his family work. When you take these factors into consideration, it's no wonder that people can relate to Donald.

"He's no politician. He's a businessman. He knows how to talk. He can give an hour speech without notes." Ivana added that if Donald was elected: "He'd make a decision! Obama

---

[37] https://www.biography.com/people/donald-trump-9511238

cannot make a decision if his life depends on it. It's ridiculous." Said Ivana Trump[38]

"We differed on how we looked at the world and how we wanted to raise our child," daughter Tiffany Trump, now 22), Maples got a relatively small settlement reported to be less than $2 million; she later auctioned off her engagement ring and other items to generate funds. "People saying, 'He pays her not to talk about him?' – that's not true," Maples says. "I feel very blessed for how my life is, but I do have to laugh when people think I walked away with a fortune." Said Marla Maples[39]

The real Donald is not what is portrayed in the media. He is a human being. Even though he is a billionaire, he is not out of touch with the struggles that the average American family has had to endure.

Consider the following well known but under reported facts:

Donald sheltered Jennifer Hudson rent free after her family was murdered.[40]

---

[38] http://www.usmagazine.com/celebrity-news/news/ivana-trump-gives-rare-interview-about-donald-trump-talks-affair-w201202

[39] http://people.com/tv/marla-maples-opens-up-about-life-after-split-from-donald-trump/

[40] http://people.com/celebrity/donald-trump-shelters-jennifer-hudson/

Donald sued the City of Palm Beach when he brought a segregated club. Mar a Lago to open it to Jews and Blacks.[41]

Donald paid to ensure a Mexican American boy would graduate from college when he saw a news story about his terminally ill mom. [42]

Donald dispatched his plane to fly a sick Jewish boy for special care when he heard no airline would accommodate his medical equipment.[43]

Donald sent $10,000 to hero bus driver Darnell Barton after seeing a news story about how he saved a woman from jumping off a bridge.[44]

Donald gave the job of constructing Trump Tower to Barbara Res, making her the first woman in history to build a skyscraper.[45]

---

[41] https://www.washingtonpost.com/politics/inside-trumps-palm-beach-castle-and-his-30-year-fight-to-win-over-the-locals/2015/11/14/26c49a58-88b7-11e5-be8b-1ae2e4f50f76_story.html?utm_term=.cbfa7c88c0c1

[42] http://thehill.com/blogs/ballot-box/presidential-races/274624-ex-miss-wisconsin-tears-up-thanking-trump-at-rally

[43] Rabi, Yitzhak. "Orthodox Child with Rare Ailment is Rescued Aboard Tycoon's Jet." *Jewish Telegraphic Agency*. 20 July 1988.

[44] http://buffalonews.com/2013/11/07/bus-driver-receives-trump-check-headed-for-rachael-ray-show/

[45] https://news.google.com/newspapers?nid=1291&dat=19801225&id=2ggyAAAAIBAJ&sjid=K40DAAAAIBAJ&pg=6833,5204145&hl=en

Are these the behaviors of someone who does not care about people?

Donald is approachable. This is a character trait that those who are in power in political circles do not have. Because Donald remained grounded, he is not out of touch with the people. For a long time the elites have caused us to feel as if we have done something wrong as Americans. We endured Barack's apology tours around the world where Barack traveled around apologizing to other nations because we were blessed to be bigger, stronger and have a better quality of life.

Mr. Obama told the French (the French!) that America "has shown arrogance and been dismissive, even derisive" toward Europe. In Prague, he said America has "a moral responsibility to act" on arms control because only the U.S. had "used a nuclear weapon." In London, he said that decisions about the world financial system were no longer made by "just Roosevelt and Churchill sitting in a room with a brandy" -- as if that were a bad thing. And in Latin America, he said the U.S. had not "pursued and sustained engagement with our neighbors" because we "failed to see that our own progress is tied directly

to   progress   throughout   the Americas."[46]

Contrast this with Donald...

Speaking in broad generalities, Trump said he would disown Obama's "apology tour," instead working to "proudly promote our system of government and our way of life as the best in the world – just like we did in our campaign against communism during the Cold War. We will show the whole world how proud we are to be American."[47]

Isn't it odd that every other nation can have a heritage, history, ancestry, and culture that they are proud of but America is not allowed to have this type of pride? The Elites have portrayed this type of pride as arrogance. Arrogance means to have informal big-headedness or vain glory. Vain glory means to have inordinate pride in oneself or one's achievements.

This nation was built on the principles of rugged individualism. It was built on the ideal that an individual can work really hard and make something of them. This produces a sense of value to the individual that is not manufactured through word or classes but it comes from accomplishing a task. The elites of this nation have no idea

[46] http://www.rove.com/article/the-presidents-apology-tour--16057
[47] http://www.dailywire.com/news/8954/trump-no-more-apology-tourwe-will-show-whole-world-ben-shapiro#

what this means and studies have shown that if something is given to an individual they will appreciate it far less than if they worked for it themselves. This is an old biblical principle.

> **2 Thessalonians 3:10 {AMP}**
> [10] For even while we were with you, we used to give you this order: if anyone is not willing to work, then he is not to eat, either.

> **Proverbs 26:13-16 {NKJV}**
> 13 The lazy man says, "There is a lion in the road!
> A fierce lion is in the streets!"
> 14 As a door turns on its hinges,
> So does the lazy man on his bed.
> 15 The lazy man buries his hand in the bowl;
> It wearies him to bring it back to his mouth.
> 16 The lazy man is wiser in his own eyes
> Than seven men who can answer sensibly.

These are Christian principles that this nation must return unto. The deceptiveness of evil is that this method does not seem compassionate. This methodology for dealing with citizens and having a productive society is contrary to the school of thought of the elites. The masses have transitioned from having a strong work ethic to one of a non-work ethic. We discussed this in Chapter 2; we talked about how people would rather receive than give.

You can be mad at Donald's father for giving him a small loan. The truth of the matter is that Donald took the 5 talents that he was given and turned them into 10. When you read this passage in **Matt 25: 14 – 30**, God was mad at the person who did nothing with what he had.

> **Matthew 25:24-28 (NKJV)**
> 24 "Then he who had received the one talent came and said, 'Lord, I knew you to be a hard man, reaping where you have not sown, and gathering where you have not scattered seed. 25 And I was afraid, and went and hid your talent in the ground. Look, there you have what is yours.'
> 26 "But his lord answered and said to him, 'You wicked and lazy servant, you knew that I reap where I have not sown, and gather where I have not scattered seed. 27 So you ought to have deposited my money with the bankers, and at my coming I would have received back my own with interest. 28 Therefore take the talent from him, and give it to him who has ten talents.

God was angry with the one who did nothing with what he was given. Donald has used this principle all his life. Whether he knew it or not is another story. However, you cannot be mad at him because you as an individual can do the same thing. The elites want to take from the rich and give to the poor that refuse to work. This plan has been proven to not work. It always backfires.

Donald does not fit into anyone's mold. He is his own man. He knew what he wanted and he went after it. The elites cannot stand him because they cannot pull him, sway him, or turn him to do anything that they want to do. This nation's way of doing things works. It makes sense. It's been tested and it's true. The reality is that other

American's know this and value our way of life. They see that it works.

These principles come from our Jewish brothers and sisters. We adopted and borrowed these principles from them. America is great because this nation was founded on mutual respect and love for the Jewish people.

> **For too long, scholars have ignored Columbus' grand passion: the quest to liberate Jerusalem from the Muslims.**
>
> **During Columbus' lifetime, Jews became the target of fanatical religious persecution. On March 31, 1492, King Ferdinand and Queen Isabella proclaimed that all Jews were to be expelled from Spain. The edict especially targeted the 800,000 Jews who had never converted, and gave them four months to pack up and get out.**
>
> **The Jews who were forced to renounce Judaism and embrace Catholicism were known as "Conversos," or converts. There were also those who feigned conversion, practicing Catholicism outwardly while covertly practicing Judaism, the so-called "Marranos," or swine.**
>
> **Tens of thousands of Marranos were tortured by the Spanish Inquisition.**

They were pressured to offer names of friends and family members, who were ultimately paraded in front of crowds, tied to stakes and burned alive. Their land and personal possessions were then divvied up by the church and crown.

Recently, a number of Spanish scholars, such as Jose Erugo, Celso Garcia de la Riega, Otero Sanchez and Nicholas Dias Perez, have concluded that Columbus was a Marrano, whose survival depended upon the suppression of all evidence of his Jewish background in face of the brutal, systematic ethnic cleansing.[48]

This piece of history has been hidden for quite some time by the elites. Columbus left Spain because they were being systematically destroyed by the antichrist spirit in Europe. Columbus and the first colonists came to this land because they were being slaughtered; they were seeking freedom from religious persecution. This land (our nation) became a safe haven for all people and despite what the revisionist history writers say this nation has always had a covenant with God to be a safe haven for the Jews.

Over the past eight plus years the leaders of this nation have allowed the antichrist spirit to keep us from maintaining this covenant. This sin of breaking covenant

---

[48] http://www.cnn.com/2012/05/20/opinion/garcia-columbus-jewish/index.html

with Israel, the sins of the leaders in the Church, and the sins of the leaders in the government of this nation are compiling and there shall be a day of reckoning. We shall be held accountable for everything this nation has done, especially what we have done to Israel. It's a well-documented fact that when we turn our back on them God turns His back on this nation.

Former President George W. Bush started the notable trend of harming Israel. Look at his remarks prior to Hurricanes Katrina and Rita.

> **This is a very hopeful period. Again, I applaud Prime Minister Sharon for making a decision that has really changed the dynamics on the ground, and has really provided hope for the Palestinian people. My vision, my hope, is that one day we'll see two states - two democratic states - living side-by-side in peace.**[49]

Bush stood in agreement for a two-state solution and through our pressure we forced Jewish residents in the Gaza strip to leave their land as it was returned to the Palestinians. Hurricanes Katrina & Rita were direct results of this nation breaking covenantal agreements with them and as they lost lives because we came against them, we lost lives through the plagues that were unleashed upon this nation.

---

[49] https://watch.org/eye-to-eye/incredible-parallels-between-israel-and-us-evacuations-bill-koenig

Our nation continued the trend under Barack as he snubbed them openly and publicly before the world. The antichrist spirit within Barack cannot stand the Jewish nation of Israel. Barack allowed for a photo of himself to be released to the newspapers. The picture showed him sitting at his desk with his feet in plan site. It was announced that the photo was taken of Barak while he was on the phone with Prime Minister Benjamin Netanyahu.

It is considered an insult in the Arab world to show the sole of your shoe to someone. It is not a Jewish custom necessarily, but Israel feels enough a part of the Middle East after 60 years to be insulted too.

Was there a subliminal message intended from the White House to Netanyahu in Jerusalem, who is publicly resisting attempts by Mr. Obama and Secretary of State Hillary Clinton to force Israel to stop any kind of settlement activity in occupied territories once and forever?

Whether or not it is true, it shows the mood in Israel. They feel cornered. The reactions out of Israel reflect that feeling.[50]

This was a clear insult to our allies.

---

[50] http://www.cbsnews.com/news/some-israelis-insulted-by-obama-picture/

But Mr. Obama was less inclined to be so conciliatory. He immediately presented Mr. Netanyahu with a list of 13 demands designed both to end the feud with his administration and to build Palestinian confidence ahead of the resumption of peace talks. Key among those demands was a previously-made call to halt all new settlement construction in east Jerusalem.

When the Israeli prime minister stalled, Mr. Obama rose from his seat declaring: "I'm going to the residential wing to have dinner with Michelle and the girls."

As he left, Mr. Netanyahu was told to consider the error of his ways. "I'm still around," Mr. Obama is quoted by Israel's Yediot Ahronot newspaper as having said. "Let me know if there is anything new."[51]

Donald has a love for the Jewish people and this translates into deep respect. He would never do anything like this. God has allowed Donald to repair the relationship with Israel and begin to restore the damage that occurred through Barack. Donald is on assignment

---

[51] http://www.telegraph.co.uk/news/worldnews/northamerica/usa/barackobama/7521391/Obama-snubbed-Netanyahu-for-dinner-with-Michelle-and-the-girls-Israelis-claim.html

from God to be used to help the nation of Israel in this season. Eventually even our nation will turn our back on Israel but it is good to know that we are safe from the blatant disrespect that Barack committed. However, the day is coming when all will abandon Israel even this nation.

> **Romans 11:25-27 {NKJV}**
> 25 For I do not desire, brethren, that you should be ignorant of this mystery, lest you should be wise in your own opinion, that blindness in part has happened to Israel until the fullness of the Gentiles has come in.
> 26 And so all Israel will be saved, as it is written:
> "The Deliverer will come out of Zion,
> And He will turn away ungodliness from Jacob;
> 27 For this is My covenant with them,
> When I take away their sins."

There are many signs, wonders and miracles in this end time hour. God has raised up Donald to fulfill a specific works and a lot of the prophets believe this works has to do with strengthening America but I believe that Donald is here to help strengthen Israel. Things have been shifting and moving in the Spirit realm since Israel was reborn in 1948.

> **Acts 3:19-21 (NKJV)**
> 19 Repent therefore and be converted, that your sins may be blotted out, so that times of refreshing may come from the presence of the Lord, 20 and that He may send Jesus Christ, who was preached to you before, 21 whom heaven must receive until the times of

restoration of all things, which God has spoken by the mouth of all His holy prophets since the world began.

We are in the times of restoration of all things. Jesus Christ is being preached to the entire world. There are reports that Jews and muslims alike are having great visitations and giving their hearts to the Lord God Jehovah. God is moving in this earth and this nation will have a part to play in this. In order for this to happen there are sins that we must repay. Because God is good; He has provided a ram for Himself. You may not like this but that Ram is Donald. Look at the what and the who was found in the Bible codes.

> **"In two separate sets of Bible Codes, published three months apart, international Bible Codes expert Rabbi Matityahu Glazerson found evidence that Donald J. Trump will win the upcoming US presidential election. What's more, Trump's predicted win appears to be connected to his support for Israel.**
>
> **The first table was published on July 6, 2016. In this table, which comes from the Book of Deuteronomy, Rabbi Glazerson pointed to the word Donald, spelled in Hebrew letters, next to the word nasi, which is Hebrew for president. He also found an abbreviation for Artzot haBrit, which**

is the way the United States is referred to in Hebrew.

The date is also found in this table. Specifically, Rabbi Glazerson pointed out the codes for 8 Cheshvan 5777. This is the date on the Hebrew calendar that corresponds to November 9, 2016 – the first date Trump would be President-elect of the United States, if he wins the election.

The second video, released in late October, repeats many of the same codes that were found in the July video. However, these codes were found in the Book of Numbers. The first sets of codes were found in the Book of Deuteronomy.

Rabbi Glazerson opens the video with what he calls "the best meeting" of Donald Trump, spelled in Hebrew, and bocher, which means chosen or elected. In this table as well, he found codes for nasi (president), Artzot haBrit (United States) and 7 Cheshvan 5777, which corresponds to Tuesday, November 8, 2016, which is Election Day in the US. All these codes appear very close to one another in the table.

In another part of the table, he found ohev Yisrael which means one

**who loves Israel. There are also codes
for teshuva (repentance), Moshiach
and Hashem Elokecha (The Lord your
God), which Rabbi Glazerson said is "a
message for Jews."**[52]

Taking all of this evidence into account one can
clearly see that Donald was chosen by God to do something
for God and for the nation of Israel. The Bible codes are
remarkable. It showed how this election played out and
proved that it doesn't matter what people say about you.
When God says you are the Victor, you are not a joke.

---

[52] https://www.breakingisraelnews.com/77884/bible-codes-predict-trump-win/#wadhzZ1UjHMuBsJt.97

8

A Civil War is Brewing

We have seen this tumultuous race rock our country backwards and forwards, left and right. This race has had many shocking ups and downs. We had everything from e-mail scandals to wars within the parties. No matter how you stacked it up people were upset. We had the media heavily involved in this race and they claimed to not have a bias. Their bias came out in extreme ways. They ignored many criminal acts committed by Hillary and the slightest etiquette faux paus made by Donald caused him to be treated on the same level as him committing a murder. People have been unfair on all levels of this election.

Taking everything into account we have discussed so far we must acknowledge how great our God is. We must acknowledge the length's the He will go through to cause His plan to take place.

What Now?   Many are still asking this question. Many are still trying to fathom what happened.   Why did Hillary lose?   There was such an anger that erupted from the supporters of Hillary that demonstrations immediately ensued and have not stopped.   Women were angry and took to the streets to protest Donald.   There were people who came out and said that Donald was not their president. This is unprecedented.

The media contributed to this anger and continues to give an open platform to those who did not agree with the election results.   Every kind of conspiracy theory came to the forefront.   The worst of which was that middle class white males spoke loud and clear against the policies that Barack had put in place.   It was no secret that Hillary was going to continue to these policies despite how it was crippling this nation.

This nation has been divided since Barack took office in 2008.   This division is growing and as the election results came in the evidence of hatred against righteousness was stupendous.   The hatred for righteousness grew.   We are even more living in the days where good is called evil and evil is called good.

> **Isaiah 5:20 {AMP}**
> 20 Woe (judgment is coming) to those who call evil good, and good evil; Who substitute darkness for light and light for darkness; Who substitute bitter for sweet and sweet for bitter!

Everything negative that could be dredged up against Donald was done. These so called disqualifying events that the media provided did not sway the American people from voting their heart. Donald promised if he were elected that he would **"Drain the Swamp and Make America Great Again!"** His message resonated with the hearts of the American people. White and black Americans, his message even resonated with the leader of the Nation of Islam, Louis Farrakhan.

> **"Farrakhan said Obama is not a true leader, but merely a stooge of white establishment Democrats who ignore the plight of struggling African-Americans.**
>
> **"I visited the worst neighborhoods [in Chicago]. I talked to the gangs. And while I was out there they said 'You know, Farrakhan, the president ain't never come here. Could you get him to come and look after us?'"**
>
> **Farrakhan continued: "If you can't go and see them, then don't worry about your legacy because the white people that you served so well, they'll preserve your legacy. But you didn't earn your legacy with us. We put you there."**
>
> **Farrakhan also slammed the Democratic Party, saying it has made empty promises to help the African-American community but delivered nothing:**

"So you Democrats, you been their [African-American] party a long time. What did you get? You got a president who's worried about his legacy. You want Hillary to get in to protect your legacy because Trump said the minute he gets in, he is going to reverse the Affordable Care Act. Because that is your signature achievement."

Farrakhan continued: "There's your legacy, Mr. President: It's in the streets with your suffering people."

As the leader of a non-profit organization, Farrakhan cannot "endorse" a political candidate without jeopardizing the Nation of Islam's tax exempt status.[53]

Farrakhan was not a friend or fan of Hillary and there are hours upon hours of him actively campaigning against Hillary and Barack. The point is clear. Trump had a message and it was received by everyone. Race did not matter. This election was about ideology.

When you look at this nation and the things our leaders have done to us. There is no reason for the policies being put in place that have been put in place. Except for one clear goal, they were **all** designed to cripple this nation. They were designed by people controlled by the

---

[53] http://www.theimproper.com/142510/muslim-louis-farrakhan-obama-failed/

antichrist spirit so that this nation would be brought down to its knees from the inside out.

Our leader's policies on the economy, on health care, and on the environment, are crippling our nation and there is no reason for the people in this land of opportunity to be suffering.   Donald promised to get the oppressive government of the backs of the people of this nation. He started immediately and he is not going to quit until he finishes. The elites of this nation had to eat a lot crow but they are not giving up easily. They are deeply embedded and they are making war from within.

You may or not be aware of this but we have two houses that are fighting against each other in our political system today.

> **2 Samuel 3:1 {NKJV}**
> 3 Now there was a long war between the house of Saul and the house of David. But David grew stronger and stronger, and the house of Saul grew weaker and weaker.

We have the **house of Saul** being represented by Barack and Hillary and their supporters versus the **house of David** being represented by Donald and his supporters.

We are in the middle of a war that we should not be fighting. The house of Saul is working behind the scenes to hinder the agenda of the house of David. What was not clear to me were some things that the antichrist spirit is still doing behind the scenes because of this election and in this nation. This leads me to believe that there is a bigger agenda going on here. Something much more powerful than just what mere human minds can work. It is an agenda that is tied together, with the antichrist system that has already begun taken over this world and this nation.

Say what you will but the powers that are not wholly and fully in love with Jesus Christ are swiftly working behind the scenes to undermine and completely sink this nation into the abyss that is the pro-homosexual and antichrist movements. Never before in our lifetime can people who are so in love with communistic ideas and thoughts be elevated to such high plateaus in the public eye. Not only are they elevated to these positions but they remain in them wreaking their havoc and destruction on all that is Godly. Something has been lost. It used to be evil to be a communist. It used to be evil to think red, but when you look deep into the heart of the people who associate and identify Hillary and Barack something just does not line up.

There is an aligning of the principalities and powers of gog and magog with the antichrist spirit. This alignment has already taken place in Europe and is moving swiftly behind the scenes in the rest of the world. This same spirit allowed for the extermination of millions of Jews in Europe. I find it interesting to note that the Radical muslim extremists love Hitler and what he stood for. The Apostle John saw the antichrist spirit and its destructive nature and he called it what it was. Not so in todays 'we have to love everybody church'. Evil is not called what it is and many are falling prey to the deception that is Islam.

If you don't believe that gog and magog are tied together with the antichrist spirit, you need to dig deeper in your word. These two principalities (gog, magog and the antichrist Spirit) are friendly to each other. Do you realize that France, England, and Spain are being overtaken by radical muslims? Do you realize that these same radical muslims do not want to follow European laws anymore, they have brought in their own law (Sharia) and the not so wise Europeans have agreed to let them do this? I can understand why they agreed, they don't want their country destroyed.

Study your Bible; we are waiting for some signs to occur here in this nation in regards to the war of gog and magog. This war does not take place in our hemisphere. These signs are not happening here, they are occurring over in Europe and the Middle East. These spiritual forces of darkness have aligned themselves and they are on the move. Do you honestly believe that these forces have not been aligning themselves here in this nation? Don't be deceived the radical muslims are here and there are communists that have rooted themselves within this nation's government and at the strategic time they will show themselves again.

Isn't it strange that Barack and Hillary's supporters have ties to many terrorist organizations, Louis Farrakhan, former Libyan President Moammar Khadafi, Jeremiah Wright, and William Ayers? Isn't it even stranger that after the days of '911' where the American people swore that 'we would never forget' that the American Press gives them a free pass on the issue? What is really going on? I believe that we are being led to the slaughter, the real silence of God's lambs. Don't talk about muslims! Don't talk about homosexuals! Don't talk about sin! Don't judge! Don't have discernment! Don't warn people to get right and repent! Don't call 'evil' evil! Don't stand for righteousness! Don't stand for holiness! Stand for sloppy agape! Stand for loose grace! Stand for peace and unity! I must tell you that based upon patterns in the Old Testament, God's judgment has come to this nation.

The top leaders in the Church today did seek the face of God concerning this election but a mixed message was delivered to the people. This mixed message did not give a clear signal to the Body of Christ. This nation was allowed to go into darkness in past elections because the leaders could not gain the mind of the Lord. There is corruption in our priesthood and this bringing forth our own judgment. Prior to this election we were on a track to harm Israel. Because Donald was elected this has been postponed. Please be do not be lulled into a place of complacency. There will be an even greater tendency to relax our guard and this is dangerous. Former President George W. Bush was a strong Christian and loved Israel too but even he was used to harm Israel. We have to be vigilant.

What the body of Christ is failing to understand is that the Jewish people are coming out of their season of punishment. It's important that you understand this; it will revolutionize your walk with Christ. God is turning His heart back to His people because their period of punishment is about over. You see right now, we have this gentile pride thing going on thinking that God must move amongst us, He must have His power fall upon us.

We need to be watchful of this saints because the Bible gives a clear warning to the gentile church in **Romans 11**. If you read it in the spirit, it will scare you, because you will see that right now, the gentile body of Christ is hanging on by a thin thread. The gentile body of

Christ thinks that it's alright but it's really in a mess. The Church doesn't have a covenant that we can fall back on outside of Jesus Christ. The part that's really scary is what is going on in the Middle East. The Jews and the Muslims are having visions of Jesus Christ and they are giving their heart over to the Lord.

And the numbers of them that are turning to Christ are increasing daily. When I think about Paul and some of the things that He wrote to the Gentile Church, about how in the end time there would be a great falling away, how the love of many would wax cold, how lawlessness would abound and increase the more and more. When I think about the fact that Paul was called to and talking to the Gentile Church that puts a little question in my spirit. What really is about to happen to the gentile Body of Christ?

Are some of them going to be lost forever? Let's face it; with the exception of the remnant in the gentile church, the gentile church has been lulled to sleep. The Gentile church thinks that it's OK; the Gentile Church cannot endure the truth of the Gospel. The Gentile church is still sucking on the milk out of the bottle, when it should be on the meat of the Word. What's it going to take for the Gentile church to wake up? And how many have to die and bust the gates of hell wide open before the rest of the gentile church wakes up.

Romans 11:25-29 {NKJV}
25 For I do not desire, brethren, that you should be ignorant of this mystery, lest you should be wise in your own opinion, that blindness in part has happened to Israel until

> the fullness of the Gentiles has come in.
> ²⁶ And so all Israel will be saved, as it is written:
> "The Deliverer will come out of Zion,
> And He will turn away ungodliness from Jacob;
> ²⁷ For this *is* My covenant with them,
> When I take away their sins."
> ²⁸ Concerning the gospel *they are* enemies for your sake, but concerning the election *they are* beloved for the sake of the fathers. ²⁹ For the gifts and the calling of God *are* irrevocable.

I want to show you something here in **verse 29**, I want you to see how good our God is...

We take this scripture to mean one thing and I think that God has something a little different that He wants us to understand about this scripture. The Jews are going to be reestablished. The covenant that they have is going to be reinstated. God is a man of His word, because He made a promise to Abraham and not only that but Abraham was found by God to be Righteous in all of his ways. Because of the Righteousness of one man, the Jews shall be saved. Because the righteousness of one man the whole world has a chance to receive salvation. This doesn't mean they will take it but it does mean they have the chance.

Because of the Righteousness of one man, Because God cannot lie to Abraham the Jews will be re-grafted back into the Vine and made a people strong and mighty in God. That's totally awesome. And this ought to tell us that if we are faithful and righteous to God, the same promises that He promised them will come to pass in our lives, no matter how long it takes God to fulfill it. That ought to encourage you to continue to press in to the fight, continue to wage war with your flesh, with the Devil with whoever you have to maintain the promise that God has given you.

God has an agenda. There is nothing that you can do to stop it. There is no prayer, no fast, and no amount of screaming and hollering that can change the course of this world. It will be as God desires it to be. The bigger picture is that the Gentile dispensation is still drawing to a close. The amount of people receiving their salvation still needs to increase and we really need to refocus on what God would have us to do.

If the truth were to be understood by the Gentile Body of Christ it didn't matter who the next President was going to be, judgment has come to this nation. This will not be averted anymore. God put Donald in the White House to fulfill God's purposes towards Israel. The church is going to go through a major shift.

What really matters is that the lethargy is increasing in the church and the Church needs to address this. The spirit of division has crept in to the Gentile Body of Christ. The 'secret' racists are coming out of the closet in the church left and right. We will see the anger of the Lord come on the scene because of the sin of reverse racism that remains in the pulpits. How can we secretly harbor these racist attitudes and expect to occupy a space in heaven? I long for the day when there will be no color barrier in the church but as long as this secret sin abides in the hearts of the black, hispanic, and white leaders in the church it will continue to be a stench in the nostrils of God.

I do believe that God has shown us who the real children of God are through this election. They are the ones who are silently praying and listening for Gods instruction. They are not caught up in the hype that went on. They were praying and interceding with God that maybe one more time God would have mercy on this country.

Those who are walking in the spirit can see what God is about to do. They can see that it is not going to be pretty. They can see that many will die just like in Noah's day. God has been telling us to step into His ark but very few have prepared themselves for this journey. Once the judgment of God has been fully unleashed there will be no opening of the ark door. You will not be able to open the door and get into the safety of the Ark. It has to be done now. But alas the church still sleeps, like nothing is happening. The church still continues to meddle in the things of God.

In everything that God does there is a plan. I happen to think as the judgments of God continue to be poured out across this land, I believe that the Church in this nation is going to be propelled into one the greatest revivals this world has ever seen. I am excited to be a part of this and you should be also.

The REMNANT is hungering and thirsting after God like never before.

The REMNANT may be small in number but they are going to be like the 5 wise virgins, they are going to be ready to reap the harvest and they are going to work with the Lord to bring it in.

The REMNANT is not scared of the judgments that are coming because they have been eagerly awaiting the Glory of God. God has been telling us since way before 2007 that His Glory was coming. He even told my Pastor to not grow weary in telling the people that it is coming.

Isaiah 10:20-23 {NKJV}
20 And it shall come to pass in that day
That the remnant of Israel,
And such as have escaped of the house of Jacob,
Will never again depend on him who defeated them,
But will depend on the LORD, the Holy One of Israel, in truth.
21 The remnant will return, the remnant of Jacob,
To the Mighty God.
22 For though your people, O Israel, be as the sand of the sea,
A remnant of them will return;
The destruction decreed shall overflow with righteousness.
23 For the Lord GOD of hosts
Will make a determined end
In the midst of all the land.

The judgments that are coming to this earth are going to bring fear into the hearts of man. As the REMNANT, we have nothing to fear. You may not believe this but we want this to happen. The world doesn't respect the Church anymore. Once these judgments start occurring the fear of God will return to all peoples. They will know by the anointing that the Church is covered by God and that God is with us. This is the good type of fear, the Bible says that the fool says in their heart that there is no God, and there are many fools walking around on the face of the earth right now.

If you look at the things that have happened it's our fault. It's because of our sin against God that the hedge of protection has been removed from us and it's our sin that will keep that hedge of protection from coming back up. We just read a crystal clear word from the Lord demonstrating what God will do When He does not get the Holiness and purity that He demands from the people who claim to love Him. You need to stop and think why New Orleans, Mississippi, and the rest of the Gulf States were totally blown away by Hurricane's Katrina and Rita.

Stop and think about all the wildfires that are breaking out all over the country. Stop and think about the severe drought that we are in. Stop and think about the crops that have been destroyed by severe weather in the United States. Doesn't this sound like God is upset with His people in this nation? We are getting ready to go into one the most dangerous times ever in the history of mankind. And it's all because people think that they know better than God... The days ahead are going to be dark and gloomy but you must remember one thing. It would be better for you to go through and persevere this right now, than to deny Christ and be eternally banished to Hell forever.

God has been warning the Church for years. What's sad is that many "Revivals" have come and gone. Many produced great works. Many ended in shame because the enemy came in and used the Church to shut these things. I know that Gods heart is for us. I know that at times the message from the Church is mixed but don't allow that to stop you from doing and being His son or His daughter.

Revival is coming and God is gonna be moving with some good things as well as some bad. If we heed Him and allow for this process to be completed it will work out for our good. If we don't it will be utter destruction.

CONCLUSION
It's His Agenda Not Ours

> **Proverbs 25:2 {NKJV}**
> [2] *It is* the glory of God to conceal a matter,
> But the glory of kings *is* to search out a
> matter.

I want you to know that even though all Hell is about to break loose. This Hell is not because of Donald. It's here to bring us into Revival and provoke Israel to serve God. God is still in control. It is my hope that this book answered some of the questions that were burning on your heart. Looking up close it's hard to imagine how we got here but looking at things from afar we can learn and see that this has been brewing for a long time.

All of our lives are about to change. In some ways they are gonna get harder and in other ways we are going to experience the Glory of God like never before. When your friends come to you disgruntled and dismayed at Donald remember that if Hillary would have won things would have degraded beyond repair.

He is still moving and working out His plan for this End-Time hour. It is my hope that you take this opportunity and become more secure in God. We are still trying to understand all that will happen as a result of these elections. We can't go back, we can only go forward. You need to see that God allowed this outcome to propel us forward as a nation and bring about some much needed course corrections for this nation.

If you are one of those people who didn't see or perceive what was going on. Don't allow yourself to go down prophetically. Take the time to get before the Lord and seek Him even more. This doesn't mean your gifting and ministry should be shut down. There are some things that God did not reveal to everyone. You still have people that God has assigned you to minister to. Minister to them, be honest with them and tell them the truth. You will earn their respect and trust.

For those of you who heard right and endured a lot of suffering. Lift your Brothers and Sisters up. Don't get into pride and arrogance. Stay humble and walk softly before God's people. There is more work that is going to use you to do and you don't want to disqualify yourself by getting into sin. We are on the verge of one of the greatest moves of God ever.

We have a lot of work to do. Praise God for everything that He has shown us. It's not too late to draw yourself closer to Him. Now is the time, now is the day of salvation. Now is the day of the vengeance of our God. He is sending His son and His angelic army to set things right. The blood of the innocents are crying out for justice. They are about to receive that which they have longed for, eternal peace.

It is only going to get uglier from here. More lies, more deception, more death and destruction. This is a major principality and power at work here. This one will be a sign to all of God's true people so they know that the end is near. These are the days of Elijah. And Elijah had a real enemy; a demonic principality and power structure that went by the name of ahab and jezebel. Seduction was the number one tool used by this enemy. It is being used now. Don't fall.

Selah

WHO THIS IS ALL ABOUT?

Romans 14:11-12 {NKJV}
11 For it is written:
"As I live, says the Lord,
Every knee shall bow to Me,
And every tongue shall confess to God."
12 So then each of us shall give account of
himself to God.

Hebrews 9:27-28 {NKJV}
27 And as it is appointed for men to die once,
but after this the judgment, 28 so Christ was
offered once to bear the sins of many. To
those who eagerly wait for Him He will appear
a second time, apart from sin, for salvation.

I realize that these truths may have shaken you to your core. I want to leave you with some hope. Not in me, but in my Savior, Jesus Christ. He died for me. He paid the price for my sins and He paid the price for yours.

Everything in this life is going to pass away. It all will be destroyed. We are destined to stand before our maker in eternity. In this life you are presented with a choice; to accept Him as your Lord and Savior or reject Him and forever be banished into Hell with the devil and his angels. You can open your heart to Him right here right now.

When you do this, you will never be alone again. His presence shall come into you and you shall be born again of the Spirit. You shall inherit eternal life because you will be an heir of His righteousness. You don't have to live in fear of the future. You can live in the love of the Father. He is waiting for you, call on Him today.

> **Romans 10:13 {NKJV}**
> 13 For "whoever calls on the name of the Lord shall be saved."

Call upon Him today and receive the free gift that God the Father has for you.

Pray this and receive Him today

"Father, I know that I have broken your laws and my sins have separated me from you. I am truly sorry, and now I want to turn away from my past sinful life toward you. Please forgive me, and help me avoid sinning again. I believe that your son, Jesus Christ died for my sins, was resurrected from the dead, is alive, and hears my prayer. I invite Jesus to become the Lord of my life, to rule and reign in my heart from this day forward. Please send your Holy Spirit to help me obey You, and to do Your will for the rest of my life. In Jesus' name I pray, Amen."

You can contact us for help with walking out your salvation at www.lighthousechurchinc.org/contact-us/

Christopher A. Gore, Reverend

The Lighthouse Inc., Church.

Christopher is serving the Body of Christ as Assistant Pastor with his spiritual father, Barbara Lynch (Pastor/Evangelist) at the Lighthouse Inc., Church in Wyoming, Delaware. He and wife Kathryn are raising their three children Kristopher, Andrew and Kierstyn in the ways of the Lord.

He has been serving in the house of God in various capacities from early childhood. He has a deep hunger for the Word of God and this has opened up a door for him to teach and minister in the Lighthouse Inc., Church since 1995. Under the mentorship of Evangelist Barbara Lynch, he was ordained as a minister of the Gospel in 2002.

Christopher has been assisting with teaching God's word, caring for His sheep, ministering in deliverances since 1995, and instructing at the Training Center for Exorcisms. He has taught the Body of Christ in Sunday school on adult and youth level classes on various topics of the Bible. He has been a featured speaker for many services including conferences at the Lighthouse Inc., Church. He has been on the Voice of Yahweh Radio, has written many articles and teachings from the Bible to help train and equip the Body of Christ for His service.

Christopher has a love for learning the deeper things of God's word and has a deep desire for the Body of Christ to grow in Christ.

www.ingramcontent.com/pod-product-compliance
Lightning Source LLC
Chambersburg PA
CBHW022113280326
41933CB00007B/367